To Persia, With Love

Doreen Corley

Copyright © 2012 Doreen Corley

All rights reserved.

ISBN: **1494340097**
ISBN-13: **978-1494340094**

DEDICATION

This book has been years in the making, with the cry, "Mom, have you written the book yet?!" heard many times. My son David was particularly enthusiastic about the prospect of this story being told.
One day he blurted in frustration, "Have you written the book yet? I don't want to have to write it after you've gone on to heaven!" Unfortunately, one day thereafter, at the age of 50, David had a massive stroke and went on to heaven unexpectedly. I was devastated.

A couple of years went by, and my thoughts turned to the multiple letters my mother, Betty Sutton, had saved from my 25 years in Iran. I was now in possession of said letters, and began to realize that soon I would be meeting David, and his first question would be, "Mom, did you write the book?" His three siblings were no less eager to hear about where they had grown up and what was happening in the lives of the Corley clan all those years ago.

So, with much love and affection, I'd like to dedicate this volume to David W. Corley, and to Stephen H. Corley, Timothy P. Corley, and Ruth Doreen (Corley) Foreman, as well as to our eight grandkids, Helen, Matthew, Andrew, Daniel, Joseph, John, Rebecca, and Melissa.

So all may know the goodness of the Lord through His dealings with us!

Note: While all the events and persons described in the book are factual, some names have been changed to protect privacy.

CONTENTS

	Acknowledgments	i
1	Keep in Touch With the Captain	7
2	Introduction to the Middle East	16
3	From Cornfields to Foreign Fields	28
4	Village Life	50
5	On to Hamadan!	64
6	Ins and Outs of Daily Life	88
7	Babies and Blizzards	104
8	Kohinoor: "Mountain of Light"	114
9	"I Thought We Were Coming Back to America!"	123
10	We Finally Beat the Presbyterians	132
11	Snapshots of the Life of a Boarding Mom	142
12	Going on Someone Else's Honeymoon	161
13	Tragedy Strikes	165
14	Rest and "Relaxation"	173
15	The Beginning of the End	181
	Epilogue	191

1 Keep in Touch With the Captain

Bam! The box hit the floor like a gunshot, contents scattering like shrapnel. I jolted awake and struggled to reorient myself through a fog of receding sleep. Darkness pressed in hard from all sides.

"Dick?" I sat up in bed and squinted across the tiny cabin to the bed where my husband was sleeping.

"I guess we've hit that storm," Dick said, groaning a bit as the ship heaved. "I'll go check on Stevie."

I heard him shift his legs over the bed, followed by a sharp yelp as his toes connected with something that wasn't floor.

"Well, if Stevie needs to be entertained, his Tinker toys are ready for him," Dick announced. Keeping his feet glued to the floor and wading through the Tinker toys like waves at the beach, he made his way to the next-door cabin where Stevie, our three and one-half year old son, had been put to bed hours before.

Alone in the dark, I lay back against my pillow, forcing deep breaths as lightning illuminated the room. Stevie's Tinker toys skittered across the floor from beneath Dick's bed to mine as the freighter bucked again. *I hope none of our other things have spilled in the storm.*

Considering that I felt as though I was about to spill from bed, I wasn't optimistic that the 10 steel barrels Dick and I had packed for our journey would be unharmed.

It's ok, I reassured myself. *People have been living in Iran for centuries without American stuff; surely I can learn to do the same.*

As the ship continued to jerk, I closed my eyes and tried to remember what land felt like, but the thundering voice of the storm refused to give me respite. I gripped my stomach as a wave of nausea broke over me, trying to keep my mind from flashing back to the only other experience I'd had on water. Though it had been more than 12 years ago, I could vividly remember the feel of water closing around my head as I pitched forward off the dock behind my house. A passerby had come to the rescue, but not before the fear of sailing had been eternally imparted to my soul. It was almost laughable that God had called me to start my missionary career with a several week journey across the ocean. . .almost.

Please, Lord, I thought. *Please help us reach Iran safely.*

Leaving Home

It was difficult to grasp the fact that just a few short hours before we had been chiefly concerned about not having the opportunity to sail at all. When we had first tried to board the ship a week earlier, we were turned away with the explanation that the cargo was not yet fully loaded. The freight company was more concerned with transporting the cargo than with the eight or so passengers brave or poor enough to choose to travel via freighter.

The frenzy that surrounded the packing of the ship and the exploration of our two small cabins had kept me off-kilter, and as we gathered on the deck and the motors began to purr, I felt my emotional pendulum swing from excitement to an undefinable but definite sense of loss. As the ship slid from the New York harbor, I clenched the rail in one hand and Stevie's chubby hand in the other. The harbor was positively crawling with humanity, but not a single familiar face came into view, nor could I have reasonably expected one. Everyone we knew was back home in Illinois.

I took a deep breath and blinked hard to keep the conflicted tears at bay. I was so...as far as I knew, the English language had never coined a word for the range of emotion that washed over me; excitement, hope, fear, grief, and awe all battled for top position in my emotional line-up. Despite having had several months to prepare, I still found myself unable to fathom the enormity of our decision to become missionaries to Iran.

"Wow, Lord," I murmured. *"I can't believe we're actually leaving...I'm not sure I'm ready for this."*

"I didn't call you to be ready," he reminded me. *"Just willing."*

I glanced up to see the Statue of Liberty gliding out of view. A lump gripped my throat as the finality of our move sank in. *It'll be at least five years before I see that again,* I realized, swallowing hard.

I jolted back to the present as Dick entered the room. "Stevie's fast asleep," he told me, faltering across the floor until he found his bed. He all but fell into it as the ship shuddered violently, and despite my fears I had to grin at his vexed grunt.

"You did pack some Dramamine, right?" Dick asked, and by a flash of lightning, I could see that we were essentially mirror images of one another—a pair of scared 20-somethings clutching their stomachs, faces lined with unspoken apprehension.

I clenched my jaw against my own nausea as the ship bobbled. "I did. But I haven't the faintest idea where it is." I started to chuckle at the irony, but settled for a weak grin when my stomach reacted again.

Dick mumbled something about Murphy's Law and pulled his knees to his chest.

All of my worst fears have already come true, and it's only the first night, I realized, fighting to keep down the nutmeg-flavored vegetables we'd been served for dinner. They hadn't been particularly tasty the first time. *Surely it can't get any worse than this!*

The thought was almost enough to soothe me to sleep.

Unfortunately, I was wrong.

Unending Storm

As the first hint of daylight peeped through the cabin porthole, I sat up in bed and edged along the cabin floor to peek outside, desperate to assess the enemy.

Everything I could see was the color of sleet, from the torrential rainfall that nearly obscured my vision to the swollen waves enveloping the deck. Suddenly a man staggered into my line of vision, gripping a covered tray in one hand and a thick rope secured along the side of the ship in the other.

"Honey, come see this!" I cried out, forgetting my personal fears in the face of this lunacy. Dick joined me at the porthole, and we stared as the man sloshed a path through the knee-deep water that covered the ship's deck. I marveled that even as the ship tossed and the man nearly lost his footing, he still kept an unfaltering grip on the tray.

The man had just disappeared from sight when there was a knock at the door, and Dick hurried to open it. The man we had just watched traverse the deck presented us the tray with a flourish.

"Some breakfast. It should settle your stomach," he informed us, adding, "The captain requests that you stay in your rooms until the storm has passed. It will be safer that way."

I was glad to find that the captain and I shared the same fundamental appreciation for life, and tried to put on a cheerful face as I woke Steve and set out breakfast. The tea and toast went down uncomfortably, despite our best efforts. As I watched Stevie build a city with his storm-animated Tinker toys, I could not help but wonder whether I had made the right decision.

My mind played a familiar scene from the support-raising visits Dick and I had made to various churches. After Dick explained our plan to go to Iran as missionaries, women would nearly always approach me with one question: "Are you really taking your little boy over there?" Over and over again, I had answered with breezy confidence, "Oh yes, it will be alright! The Lord will take care of us!" I had packed and prepared to that refrain in my own head, but now the fear masked by my breezy response finally began to creep in. *Will it be alright, Lord?* There had been little room for second guessing or fear in the frenzy of preparation, but now, sitting helplessly in the middle of an ocean hurricane, I felt as though I was in an incubator of doubt. Had Dick and I done the right thing? Would Stevie be ok?

"Listen, honey," Dick tried to encourage me. "The Lord has provided well for us so far. He clearly wants us here."

I blinked back tears. "He clearly wants us to come this far," I agreed. "But how much farther?"

Dick shrugged. "Well, that's up to Him, right? But that's true anywhere. That would be just as true at home in Illinois as it is right here."

"Hm. . .I suppose you're right."

I still wouldn't mind if the storm ended soon. How about tomorrow? I asked the Lord as Dick and I crawled into our tossing beds that night; in case He was open to my preferences in that moment, I wanted to be clear.

"I Don't Think We'll Ever Make it to Iran"

My hopes were unfounded. The next two days dawned savagely. The hours churned by. My resolution from the night before was breaking down in the face of cabin fever and anxiety, and all I could find to do was wander around the cabin, organizing the few things we had bothered to unpack.

The invariable meals of tea, toast, and dried beef had becoming as appealing as sea slugs, and everything about the ship was starting to aggravate me by the time I finished re-arranging and organizing the cabin for the umpteenth time in a bid to avoid the twin storms raging outside the ship and within my soul.

By noon of the third day, the cabin and I both wore matching overworked expressions, and I sat down and flipped open my Bible, looking for comfort from the ceaseless torment of my thoughts.

I found myself staring at the carefully underlined text of Deuteronomy 31.

"The Lord is the one who goes ahead of you; He will be with you. He will not fail or forsake you. Do not fear or be dismayed."

As I traced the words over and over in my mind, I recalled reading the same passage many times over the short months leading to our departure.

Those months had certainly been far from smooth-sailing, yet the Lord's hand had provided for us at every possible turn. He'd provided us with each other, with Steve, with money to go overseas; sure He would provide now, too. But was I willing to accept whatever His provision was? Even if it looked utterly unlike provision?

All right, Lord, I thought. *You brought us here, and I trust that whatever comes out of this is for the best. We trust You.*

By bedtime, as I crawled into my perpetually wobbling bunk, I had a sense of calm confidence in the Lord's way—while I knew that way would require sacrifice up front, I was convinced that the dividends would be worth it all.

As Dick cut the lights, I flipped over in bed to face him as well as I could in the thick darkness. The dark made it easier to put words to the thought that had been pounding through my head all day.

"Dick," I said softly, "I don't think we'll ever make it to Iran."

Dick was silent.

The air in the cabin held no panic, no anger, and only the barest touch of fear.

Well, Lord, I'm sure there's some purpose here, I prayed as I closed my eyes.

Whatever happens will be the greatest good. I took a deep breath and drifted slowly to sleep...

Keep in Touch with the Captain

...I startled awake and braced myself against the silence. I breathed deeply and drifted toward sleep...*Wait...silence!?!* I sat up in bed and listened hard.

"Dick!" I leaped from my bed to the porthole. "Honey! The storm is over!"

For the first time in days, there was nothing to hear except the whirring motor of the ship. The storm had ceased.

Dick sat up in bed and threw his covers to one side. "Praise the Lord!" He started to join me at the window when a knock on the door changed his trajectory. Yanking the door open, he found one of the ship's crew standing there, mercifully devoid of a tray.

"The captain would like to invite you to join him for breakfast," the man said, flashing a smile.

Dick grinned back, full of the camaraderie resulting from a shared near-death experience. "We'd be delighted!"

In just a few minutes, we joined the ship's other bedraggled travelers at the captain's table, devouring the currant buns and jam set before us and eagerly exchanging stories of the storm with our fellow travelers.

Breakfast had barely been cleared when the captain, beaming with pride, offered to take the passengers on a tour of the freighter.

"It ees one of zee finest sheeps you vill ever see," he boasted, patting the wall of his cabin affectionately.

Within moments the passengers were making their way to the bowels of the ship. Dick and I found ourselves standing by the captain, who turned an affable eye toward us.

"And how has ze treep been for you?" His blonde mustache quivered under the weight of his thick accent.

Dick and I exchanged glances. The man was so proud of his occupation that acknowledgment of our fear might seem insulting to his navigational skills—or, worse, his vessel.

"Well. . ." Dick decided to side with honesty over politeness. "It's actually been terrifying."

I nodded when the captain looked to me for confirmation. "We were terrified," I told him. "We thought we were going to die, and I was so concerned about Stevie. . ." I trailed off as the captain's expression became deeply sympathetic.

Shaking his head in consternation, he said, "I'm sorry to hear dat you vere afraid. I vish I had known—I vould have told you dat ve vere never in any danger."

I gaped at him, speechless and sheepish. *Never in any danger? All that panic, and we were never in any danger?*

Twenty minutes later, Dick and I re-entered our cabin after putting Stevie down for a nap and flopped onto our own bunks, ready for a nap ourselves.

"Well, love," Dick murmured, staring at the ceiling, "I guess the Lord wanted to start us off with a little missionary boot camp."

"I'll say! But now we've learned. When in doubt, keep in touch with the Captain!" I sighed.

It was a lesson that would serve us well for years to come.

Arrival in the Middle East

On December 5, 1955, the ship finally pulled into the Beirut harbor.

"Honey!" Dick grabbed Stevie's hand and hurried with him out to the deck. "Doreen, come look! We're in Lebanon!"

Beirut glowed in the distance like a piece of heaven. I could hardly wait to get off the ship; no piece of land had ever looked as wonderful to me as Lebanon did at that moment.

To my dismay, the passengers were not given the opportunity to disembark until the next day, and I had to resign myself to one more night on the ship. As a final gesture of goodwill, the captain called the crew and passengers together to explain that he would be throwing a Christmas party complete with traditional Dutch trappings. It was a fitting end to a long and arduous trip. The ship's occupants were giddy at the prospect of reaching land the next morning, and the chef had put particular effort into the food, which I felt was the least he could do after serving us toast for the majority of the trip.

As dinner progressed, the captain made his rounds of the table, giving each passenger a gift to honor the holiday. While he gave the other two female passengers bottles of perfume, when he reached me he handed me a beautifully scalloped silver spoon.

"Keep in touch with the Captain, Doreen," I murmured to myself as I fingered the graceful edges of the spoon. It would serve as a perfect memento of my first major missionary lesson.

As I crawled into bed that evening, I was (almost) soothed by the gentle rocking of the boat.

Tomorrow, land, I promised my travel-weary body.

2 Introduction to the Middle East

The next morning, so eagerly anticipated, dissolved into a blur. Packing the cabin was enough hassle, despite (or perhaps because of) its small size; then the barrels had to be unloaded and inspected for damage. They were then taken to a shipping company that would transfer them by truck from Beirut, Lebanon to our final destination of Kermanshah, Iran.

By the time the ship was unpacked I was eager to settle into our hotel and take a nap, and after obtaining detailed directions from a crew member to a hotel he said was both economical and safe, we took our first steps on foreign soil, alone, nervous, and excited.

The streets of Beirut were already bustling, and Steve proved to be a built-in conversation piece; his blonde hair and bright smile attracted attention from all directions as we straggled down the street.

The hotel certainly lived up to its reputation for economy. The dim light given off by the single bare bulb dangling from the ceiling of our room made it difficult to decipher whether the speckled tile on the floor was actually dirty or merely stained from decades of dust-wear.

Worn out from the busy morning and the poor sleep I had maintained over the past several weeks on the ship, I simply wanted a nap. "Come here, Stevie," I coaxed, beckoning him toward the small bed in the corner.

Stevie ran to me, giggling, but his laughter stopped short when he threw himself on the bed. "No, Mama! It *hurts*!" He frowned as he patted the rough woolen blanket.

"I know, honey." I had to admit that he had an excellent point. "But here, if you just lie down. . ."

Stevie didn't want to lie down. Stevie, ever-pleasant and perpetually energetic, had not suffered the endless nights of seasickness with which Dick and I had dealt, and he wanted to play, or at the very least, to avoid having to take a nap on the torturously rough blankets. It took all my energy and more patience than I thought I possessed to cajole him to lie down, and I found myself sighing with relief when I sank onto my own bed, rejoicing that it wasn't rolling à la the ship bunks. It felt like the first real sleep I'd had in weeks.

"Zoom!!!"

Stevie was the first of our family to finish his nap, and promptly set about the serious business of playing cars. I glanced at my watch and sat bolt upright in bed. "Oh, my! Dick, we've slept the day away!"

Dick stirred next to me. "Mmm?"

"Dick, it's 3:30 in the afternoon!"

Dick flipped over and made a sustained effort to open one eye. "Well, honey," he mumbled with as much force of logic as he could fit into his sleep-choked voice, "did you have plans for today? Tea with the queen, perhaps?"

I chuckled and smacked him playfully. "I guess not; but I've never slept that long during the daytime before. And how will we ever get to sleep tonight?"

Dick succumbed to the fact that as far as Stevie and I were concerned, his nap was over. "All right, love." He swung out of bed and picked up Stevie, rooting through our luggage for some crackers to console himself. "Why don't we get ready and go to an early dinner?"

I nodded eagerly. "I'm excited to try Middle Eastern food!"

Dick took a bite of the cracker he was holding. "What if the food here makes us ill?" He furrowed a brow.

I shrugged, amused that my food-loving husband hadn't considered this point before. "Then I guess we'll be eating flatbread at every meal for the next five years!" I rolled out of bed, snitched a piece of Steve's cracker under the guise of giving him a kiss, and headed for the bathroom to comb my hair in preparation for our first real foray into Lebanon.

Doreen Corley

Beirut: Paris of the Middle East

My senses had been dulled by exhaustion during the walk to the hotel, but as we strolled through Beirut that afternoon I found myself assailed by an overwhelming array of new sensations. The smell of exhaust and smoke hung heavily in the air, mingling with the heady scents of roasted meat and spices as we passed by markets and restaurants. The din of traffic was complemented by the chatter of arguments held at tea shops and the clatter of horse and donkey hooves as more traditional drivers fought for representation on the road. I stopped walking altogether at the sight of a man faltering down the street, bent double under the weight of the not one, but *two* refrigerators strapped to his back. "Well, we're definitely 'not in Kansas anymore'," Dick murmured to me in an undertone as we watched the man stagger around a corner and out of sight.

The stores crowded closely together along the cobbled streets, and while the Arabic script written on the signs was not particularly helpful, the shop windows, crowded with goods, made the identification of each store relatively simple. Exploration initially overtook eating in my list of priorities, but the restaurants that were generously interspersed throughout the stores soon proved too great a temptation, and Dick and I decided to find dinner, despite the relatively early hour.

Dick pulled open the door of a restaurant selected at random, and I felt a hush descend over it as I entered. Quickly dropping my eyes, I stepped aside to let Dick take the lead as a hospitable waiter bustled forward. While he did not appear to speak any English, he and Dick were able to communicate via pointing and hand signals, and we soon found ourselves seated at a plastic table, staring bemusedly at the thin plastic menus placed before us. Any attempt at deciphering the Arabic script was futile.

"Well, honey, how does this look?" I teased as I pointed out an item about half-way down the menu.

"Perfect," Dick joked back. "Let's just make sure we order one thing from each section, so we don't end up eating a plateful of desserts or 8 cups of Turkish coffee for dinner."

"As if you would object to a plateful of dessert!"

Our waiter recognized our difficulties and came to the rescue, scooping up our menus, waving away our feeble attempts to order, and indicating via gestures that he would ensure we were properly fed.

"Well, let's just hope sheep eyeballs aren't on the list of Lebanese delicacies," I said as we acceded to our waiter's hospitality and watched him disappear into the kitchen.

I needn't have worried. Within moments, the waiter emerged from the kitchen bearing a tray with large plates of flatbread, some sort of dip, and a dish full of bright red and green vegetables. He placed the large dishes on the table, handed each of us a plate, and with a combination of infinite patience and laborious repetition, finally managed to communicate to Dick that we were eating *hommas* and *tabbouleh*. While I could not identify the flavors of the dip, I noted that the *tabbouleh* salad contained tomatoes, parsley, and some kind of cracked wheat. Both the dishes and the flatbread were delicious, and even Steve was willing to munch the flatbread dipped in *hommas* without complaint. The dishes had barely been cleared away when the waiter swept them away and replaced them with something he called *kibbeh*, a fried croquette stuffed with what I thought could have been spiced ground beef.

"I may need to be more concerned with becoming overweight than getting ill," Dick said shortly thereafter as we sipped on after dinner tea and munched our dessert, little doughnut-hole-like balls in syrup called *awamat*.

I laughed. "And yet it feels so light," I pointed out, snatching an *awamat* from Stevie's grasp. I hadn't noticed the waiter slip one to the child, but given the amount of attention the little boy had garnered from the entire wait staff since we had entered the building, I was preparing myself to have a dessert scavenger hunt through his clothes when we arrived back at the hotel.

I felt comfortably affable toward the entire Middle Eastern world as we emerged from the restaurant, warmed by the hospitality of the staff and delighted with the tasty food, but that geniality ran cold as I realized that the street onto which we had just emerged looked entirely different than the one from which we had come. We had entered the restaurant during business hours, but the shopkeepers had gone home while we had lingered over our meal, and each storefront was now covered in retractable sheet metal, leaving me disoriented. I gripped Steve's hand a little more tightly as I studied the Arabic signs that I had previously overlooked, hoping one of them would trigger recognition.

"I think that one was the shoe store," Dick pointed down the road, squinting at the sign as though the English translation of the script would magically come to him.

I shook my head, uncertain. "I think it was the next one over. But regardless, it was definitely in that area, so that's a good place to start."

We made our halting way down the street, pausing every few moments to take in our surroundings and search for landmarks; the twelve minute walk to the hotel stretched into thirty, and I was relieved when we finally saw the dirty face of our hotel.

As Dick and I strolled into the bare lobby, the hotel owner rushed the meet us, chattering in Arabic. He managed to communicate via skilled pantomime that he and his family were going to be drinking tea shortly thereafter, and the Americans were welcome to join them. His insistent hospitality couldn't be refused, despite our best efforts, and Dick and I spent our first evening in the Middle East sipping tea and communicating with our kind hosts via the universal language of bewildering hand gestures.

The next few days in Beirut passed by quickly. I enjoyed exploring the beautiful old city, wandering down the cobbled side streets, and resisting the attention of vendors, who could spot a potential (and theoretically wealthy) American customer at 58 paces. Our hotel owner, who apparently had little faith in the ability of two naive Americans to navigate the city well, was prolifically cordial.

"Well, Doreen," Dick told me on one occasion as we followed the owner to the lobby for yet another round of tea and conversation with hotel guests, relatives of the hotel owner, and various other native Beirutees, "it's a good thing we like tea."

"I used to just think of it as a beverage," I agreed. "Here, it's like a national pastime!"

Thus the time in Beirut passed pleasantly enough, but Dick and I were both counting down the days until we removed to Damascus, the next of many steps toward a more permanent living situation.

"Guess what?"

I looked up from packing for the next leg of our journey to see Dick standing in the doorway wearing a smirk.

"What?" I made no effort to keep the subtext of "Uh oh" from my voice.

"I found a shared taxi to take us to Damascus." Dick's grin widened in pace with my eyes.

"Will there be room for all of us?" I gestured to the various bundles I was attempting to consolidate against all odds. I had always considered myself a good packer, but so far this trip had demonstrated ample room for improvement.

"Honey, have you *seen* the taxis here?" Dick walked over to the window and encompassed the city with a broad sweep of his arm. "If they can't find room, they make it. It's that simple."

I nodded as a reel of transportation-related culture shock played through my mind—the drivers in Lebanon appeared to prioritize speed above anything else, and safety probably didn't even rank in a top ten list of their concerns. "Yes, I suppose you're right."

And he was—shortly thereafter, I found myself perched uncomfortably between Dick and the door handle of the taxi, clutching at Steve to keep him on my lap. The two-and-a-half hour ride was primarily spent trying to decipher whether the animated speech, loud tones and overexcited gestures shared between our driver and our three fellow passengers was indicative of disagreement or appreciation of each other's viewpoints. Dick and I had still failed to reach a consensus by the time the taxi discharged us, sore and dusty, in Damascus.

Stuck in the Desert!

Our time in Damascus was short, and we only had time to visit the historical landmark turned tourist trap where Paul had been let down over the wall in Acts 9 before we purchased tickets to travel all-night across the desert to Baghdad, Iraq.

The air in the Nairn bus (a sort of bus/truck hybrid the likes of which I'd never seen before) was close, and I had barely seated myself before I was eager to disembark. Biting my lip against complaint, however, I nibbled at the sack dinner that the bus line handed out, coaxing Steve to eat his hard-boiled egg before leaning my head back against the seat for some much-needed rest.

The spluttering motor awakened me hours later.

"Dick, what's happening?" I turned my head to the right but did not have the energy to open my eyes. I heard the motor grind again as the driver tried to revive it.

"We're stuck." Dick's sleep-choked explanation left a lot to be desired.

I mustered the energy to open one gritty eye and peered outside for a landmark. There was nothing but inky blackness beyond the headlights of the bus, which in turn caught nothing but the glimmer of sand. We were stranded in the middle of the desert.

I saw the driver flick on a flashlight and a rush of cold air flooded the bus as he opened his door and hopped outside.

"Well, what now?" I knew that I had no ability to communicate with the only people who could answer that question, but I asked nonetheless.

Dick shrugged and reached over to grasp my hand. "It's alright," he assured me. "I'm sure they have some kind of system worked out to let people know we're stuck."

"Smoke signals, maybe?" I grinned weakly. I couldn't imagine how we would be able to contact the nearest city, now hours behind us, and the dearth of roads concerned me, but Dick's confidence was contagious, and I leaned my head back against my head rest and decided to wait, if only because I could think of no alternative.

The majority of the bus' male occupants were following the driver outside, and Dick decided to join them. Too tired to give much emotional support, and not being of a mechanically-minded persuasion, I closed my eyes and dozed off. Between God, Dick, and the men, who were now arguing about something of apparently seismic importance (*probably not wanting to ask directions*, I grinned sleepily to myself), surely some solution would be reached.

"Mommy?" Without warning Stevie jerked upright, looking as out of sorts as I felt. He had barely opened his mouth when a woman reached over my seat, proffering an orange, and indicated with a smile that it was for the boy. I thanked her profusely in English and smiles and quickly pacified my son with the fruit before rocking him back to sleep. When she saw Stevie was asleep, the woman leaned over yet again and gently deposited two more oranges and several hard-boiled eggs on the seat next to me, smiling and pointing to me, then outside, where Dick was standing with the men. I tried to keep the tears at bay as I smiled and strove to convey my thanks. *Ha. Here I came over to minister to the nationals, and so far, they're doing a lot more ministering to me than I am to them.* I pondered the woman's actions as I chewed on the sweet flesh of one of the oranges. I had the feeling the Persians had a lot to teach me about sacrificial generosity.

"Doreen," Dick whispered, shaking my shoulder. I squeezed my eyes tightly shut. "Doreen." Dick shook me a bit harder. "We're switching to taxis. They stopped a passing motorist, and he's gone for help."

"Oh." It was impossible to communicate much more around my sleep-fogged brain. "Fine." I handed Steve over to my husband, mumbling a heartfelt "thank you" when I realized that Dick had been up since we had gotten stuck, watching out for me and Stevie. *He has to be exhausted*, I thought as I sleepily trailed him out of the bus and into the waiting taxi. Dawn was just starting to tinge the sky a pale pink, and I had just enough light to ascertain that we truly were in the middle of nowhere. Desert sand, also stained pink by the light, surrounded us on all sides, and I felt for a moment as though I was in the midst of an Ottoman caravan. The waiting taxis quickly squelched my visions of camels and sheiks, and I slid into the taxi next to Dick. This time, however, sleep eluded me, and I watched mile after mile of sand slip past as I prayed the same prayer I had uttered hundreds, if not thousands, of times since Dick and I had recognized our call to the mission field.

Please, Lord. . .I wasn't always certain as to what specifically I was pleading for, but I figured the Lord understood. In this instance, it meant, *Please, Lord, bring us through this trip safely. . .and help us to be a blessing to others. . .and bless our time in Iran. . .and just help. . .please.*

The Lord decided to answer at least part of my prayer with a "yes." The rest of our trip was uneventful, if rather sandy, as the taxis sat lower to the ground than the bus had; it was late morning when Dick, Steve, myself, and approximately 4 pounds of sand between us were deposited outside the YMCA in the Baghdad, Iraq.

Drinking Water Meltdown

The first thing I noticed upon entering our room were the big clay pots covering the windowsill. "Oh, look, Dick. . .flowerpots?" The statement turned into a question mid-sentence as I peeked into the first one and found that it was filled with water. The other pots were likewise brimming with water, and their purpose eluded me. "I guess they decorate a little differently here," I told Dick as I flipped open the tap of the tiny room's sink to give Steve a sponge bath. I wrinkled my nose as the sulfurous water filled the room with Eau de Rotten Egg. "Ew." I bent to sniff the water and regretted it instantly. "Dick, is this water drinkable?"

"Ew!" Stevie gleefully added the word to his ever-expanding vocabulary.

"You get to take a bath in it," I informed him, pulling off his pants and emptying the sand in them out the window. Taking his cue from me,

Stevie plopped to the ground to empty his socks out onto the floor, and I was in mid-yelp when we were both distracted by a knock on the door. Dick opened it to find one of the YMCA workers holding a pot full of freshly boiled water.

"Good?" He asked, indicating the room.

Dick, by now a fluent translator of broken English, nodded enthusiastically. "Yes, yes, it's very good," he assured the man.

"I. . .show. . ." the man moved past Dick to indicate the flower pots, into which he dumped his boiling water. While Dick and I watched, he set aside his English skills and bent over to mimic the action of drinking from the trough attached to the bottom. "Good, good!" he exclaimed enthusiastically after a dramatic swallow that apparently indicated the end of the show.

"That is water for drinking?" Dick clarified.

The man nodded again. "Yes, yes!"

I was taken aback by a sense of defeat that suddenly bulldozed my emotional defenses. "I hadn't realized we would have to boil our water," I told Dick, trying to hold my tears at bay. "It's too much. . .I have to do laundry in the sink, I'm completely exhausted, there's sand everywhere, and now we have to boil our water before we could use it. . ."

Dick grabbed my hand. "You need to go to bed, love," he told me gently. "I'll give Steve a bath; you'll feel better after a nap."

"But you haven't gotten sleep either," I argued, trying to sound concerned, and chagrined to find my tone petulant.

"I have at least another half-hour's worth of work in me," Dick soothed. "I'll take a nap as soon as Stevie's cleaned up."

I was too tired to fight any further, so I gave in and collapsed into bed, trusting my husband to work everything out with the son, the sand, and the sulfur water. I awakened several hours later to find that my husband was as competent as I had believed when I'd first married him. The room and the toddler were each relatively clean, and I made it my mission to keep Stevie entertained and quiet while Dick enjoyed a very well-deserved nap.

The YMCA, though giving our hotel in Beirut serious competition for the prize of "most poorly decorated travel lodging," was tolerably clean and comfortable, and Dick and I spent the rest of our day exploring Baghdad and drinking in such sights as the Tigris and Euphrates rivers.

While I was enjoying our tour of the Middle East, I realized as I did our laundry in our small sink for the umpteenth time that I could hardly wait to get to Iran.

"Lord, You have brought us so far," I prayed aloud as I scrubbed at a stubborn sweat stain on one of Dick's shirts. "I know you'll be faithful to us the rest of the trip. . .*right?*" My heart added an addendum, against which I swallowed hard. Surely He would.

On to Kermanshah via Pilgrim Bus

The next day we finally boarded a bus headed toward Kermenshah, Iran. The bus was packed with pilgrims who had recently finished a holy journey to the city of Najaf, Iraq, and I found myself fighting to keep from staring curiously at the "ultra-holy" group of conservative Muslims who made up our fellow travelers. While I had been surrounded by Muslims since entering the Middle East, we had not met so devout a group at any point to date.

Our fellow travelers identified Dick and I as foreigners and ushered us to the best seats, directly behind the driver. I was thankful be able to tell myself that this was the final bus ride. "We're almost there, honey," I murmured in Steve's ear. Steve was oblivious to my urgency. He had grown to enjoy travel, and he plastered his nose against the window of the bus as the driver put the vehicle in gear and we rumbled out of Baghdad.

Within moments, however, Stevie cuddled up close to me as we made the unpleasant discovery that the driver had no side window shielding him from the cold winter air; thus, whatever wasn't swirling directly around him was sent back to us. I, in turn, hunkered down by Dick, occasionally pushing out my lower lip and sending a breath of warm air up toward my icy nose.

The bus was quiet for about half an hour, when it shot onto a bridge and a sudden jabber went flying up all around us from our fellow passengers. The hubbub died down as soon as we had crossed the bridge, but started up again as the bus headed for a big hill.

"I think they're saying prayers," Dick said as I tried hard not to look behind me in curiosity.

"Let's just hope they aren't saying 'Kill the foreigners,'" I replied, only half-joking as the bus reached level ground and our fellow passengers grew quiet once more.

We had been traveling for two smooth-sailing hours when the whole bus suddenly jolted as the driver floored the gas pedal. The prayers of the pilgrims increased exponentially, and I gave up trying to communicate with Dick as we braced ourselves against the floor, trying to keep from knocking our heads on each other or the ceiling as the bus bounced madly along.

I glanced out the window to see another bus creeping up beside us and realized what was happening with a jolt and a giggle. *We're racing to get to the border.* The remainder of the trip contained all the thrill of a carnival ride with none of the safety precautions. The bus shook so hard I was sure we were leaving key pieces of machinery behind; the passengers urged the driver on, Steve buried his face in my neck and sobbed, and even I felt a bit shaky when we finally pulled up to the border, victorious, to the whoops and cheers of the passengers. "I think I might need some Dramamine," I told Dick. I'd thought I'd seen the last of that particular medicine when we left the ship, but then again, I'd never met a Middle Eastern bus driver before. I pried my fingers from my seat to which (along with dear life) I had been clinging for most of the trip. Dick pulled our Dramamine out of his bag, and I had to consciously refrain from emptying the bottle—*who knows how many more of these bus rides I'll have to endure in the next five years?*

"Doctor?" A fellow passenger saw Dick offer me the medicine, and the assumptions flew; within moments, it was presumed that Dick was medical personnel.

"What do you think will happen if someone becomes seriously ill and you are not able to help them?" I asked.

"Well, let's hope they only have motion sickness, because all I have for them is Dramamine." Dick smiled.

It took hours to get through customs, but I needed that chance to decompress before the bus took off again, this time at a slower pace, into the town of Kermenshah. The driver, with typical Middle Eastern hospitality, had taken it upon himself to ensure that the foreigners were deposited safely at their destination, and we drove through town without stopping until we reached the gates of the hospital at which we would be staying during our time at Kermenshah. The gatekeeper who met us acted as translator, explaining that we could pick up our bags the next day at the bus terminal, though I was so tired I would have been willing to give the luggage up as lost forever if it meant that I could get to bed sooner.

It was 1:30 in the morning when we finally staggered out of our bus and into the home of the local American, Dr. Bussdicker. Introductions were given but barely comprehended before we crawled gratefully into bed, relieved to finally be so very close to our destination.

3 From Cornfields to Foreign Fields

Dear Mom,

We've arrived safely at the doctor's house in Kermanshah. Thank you for your prayers—with some of the difficulties we encountered, I thought we would never make it! We'll be here for a few days until Mr. McAnlis comes into town to take us out to the orphanage; I'm thankful for the chance to rest. Dr. Bussdicker has a bathtub, which is an unheard of luxury out here, and my bath this morning felt just like a piece of heaven. I woke up far too early in order to take advantage of it, and that, along with fresh clothes, has pretty much given me a new perspective on life. I might be able to survive this missionary thing after all!

It feels so surreal to be here right now—Mom, would you ever have believed that your little girl would be a missionary? In Iran, of all places?

The typewriter suddenly jammed. I sighed and jiggled the keys to reset them, but the page was already blurred, along with my letter writing motivation.

Leaning my head on one hand, I gazed out the window of the doctor's house into the courtyard of the hospital as my mind flipped back through the pages of time.

Raised in Decatur, IL, in a family hard-hit by the Depression, my life goals had been to marry, have children, and scrape out of the poverty in which I was used to living.

My childhood had been truly happy, despite the fact that my family was desperately poor; my parents loved each other and my two younger sisters deeply. While my father had to work long hours at the local soybean plant in order to make ends meet, Pat, Jackie and I were spoiled by the intangibles—the sense of having a mother who loved us and a father who was deeply proud and protective of us.

My parents were not Christians, and I probably would not have given particular thought to religion had there not been a bus that came into our neighborhood to offer rides to a Lutheran church in town. My sister Pat and I, along with two neighbor girls, decided to attend one day, probably more out of curiosity than out of a burning desire to know about Jesus. The Lutheran church became an incredible social outlet for us, as we were welcomed into their community with open arms. They also played a crucial role in my future spiritual formation, as I heard the gospel and developed a firm grasp of many biblical truths while attending that church. Despite these advantages, however, I had yet to really grasp gospel truth.

Youth Group—Meeting My Future Husband

After several years attending the Lutheran church on Sunday mornings, I added a Methodist youth meeting every Sunday night to my repertoire of church activities. My sister and I would walk the mile to youth group and have some singing and a devotional before the youth would all get together and go to the park for a walk or go out for a 5 cent hamburger at the local ice cream shop. It was on one of those nights at the youth group that I met Dick Corley. Tall, dark-haired, and bold, Dick made an interesting addition to the youth group, which was otherwise made up of town kids who had grown up together. Dick was a relatively recent addition to Decatur, having moved there with his parents a few years before. We hadn't really had a chance to get to know one another, as Dick had graduated from high school a year before me and was currently attending the local Presbyterian college.

Dick was certainly intriguing, but at that point I had just landed my first "adult" job and was too busy learning the rhythm of office work to be able to pay much attention to boys. Dick and I did, however, become acquainted over his homework; since Dick had been raised in a nominally Christian home, his grasp of Bible teachings was tenuous at best, and he would come to me with his questions.

"Hey Doreen," he would say off-handedly after a youth group meeting, "this week we talked about Jonah and the whale, and they said that it couldn't possibly be a literal story. What do you think?"

I would draw upon my Sunday school knowledge base to answer him, and thus was born our casual friendship. While I certainly was attracted to Dick, I knew that he was single-minded in his goal to finish his college degree; I therefore refused to let myself become distracted by him, and threw myself into my own schooling and social life.

Later that summer, however, Don, another youth group boy, sidled up to me during one of the meetings.

"Listen, Doreen," he started in an undertone, glancing about him nervously.

My heart sank. I liked Don, but I was not interested in going with him—even worse, I knew my sister Pat *was* interested in him. "What is it, Don?" I was determined to be gracious.

"Well, you know Dick is in the National Guard." Don shifted from one foot to another. Puzzled, I simply stared.

Don tried again. "Well, since Dick is in the National Guard, he has to go to Wisconsin for a two-week training period. And he's leaving tomorrow."

"I remember that he did that last summer, too," I said in an attempt to help him, or at least to bring the conversation to a speedier close.

"Well, he wants to write to you while he's gone. Is that all right?" Don finished in a rush, then blushed as though he had been the one to ask for communication.

I swallowed hard, giving my dignity a chance to overcome my excitement. "Why yes, Don, that would be fine," I finally managed, in the suspiciously staid tones of someone on the brink of combusting with excitement.

Don grinned at me. "Great!" Spinning around, he strode from sight, leaving me rooted to the ground, flushed and happy.

The first letter arrived three days later. I snatched it up and scurried to my room to mask my glee from the prying eyes of my sisters. Dick wrote that he had made it safely to Wisconsin and gave me some of the more interesting details of his trip. He ended with an invitation to write him back, which I promptly accepted. Over the next two weeks we exchanged several letters, and I became increasingly impatient for the day of his return.

The very day that Dick was expected back in town, my sister Pat called me shortly after dinner.

"Doreen! You have a phone call!"

I threw down my book and scurried to the receiver. "Hello?"

"Hello, is this Doreen?" The voice sounded like Dick's.

"It is." *Please be Dick, please be Dick, please be Dick.*

"This is Dick Corley."

My excitement rose, then fell in equal measure when he followed the introduction with: "I arrived back in town today, but I just got word that my grandfather passed away this week. I have to go back to my mother's farm for the funeral, and I'm leaving tonight."

"I am so sorry to hear that." I fought to contain my own disappointment as I realized how Dick must be feeling.

"I'm afraid it will be hard on Mom." Dick paused for a moment, apparently lost in his thoughts, then said, "But she isn't expecting me for another few hours, and I would like to see you before I leave. Would it be all right if Don and I came by to see you and Pat?"

"Why yes, that would be fine." I didn't bother to ask Pat about the invitation—my sister would never object to a visit from her boyfriend.

That evening went splendidly. Dick understood and played along with my lighthearted humor, yet had a streak of gravity in his character that I respected deeply. He and Don were a particularly amusing duo, and Pat and I both complained about our laughter-sore ribs as we headed to bed that night.

Dick had promised to visit me when he got back from the funeral, and I spent inordinate amounts of time over the next week wondering how he was. I did not expect to hear from him while he was gone, but that only increased my impatience to see him again.

We Both Meet Jesus

About a week after Dick had left town, he called me up to tell me he was back in town and ask if he could see me. I assented readily, and a half-hour later we were seated in my family's small living room.

"Doreen, I need to tell you something." Dick had barely greeted me before he became suddenly serious.

"What is it?" I felt a knot twist in my stomach. Something told me that whatever he was about to say was momentous.

"I accepted the Lord Jesus last night," Dick said.

I paused, trying to gauge my response. I knew what he was saying; my years in church had trained me well in Christian lingo. I had not realized that he was not a believer, but neither was I particularly surprised by the news; we had never talked about spiritual matters past his schoolwork, and I barely gave them a thought on my own. "How did that come about?" I finally asked, keeping my voice neutral.

"It started on my way home from Wisconsin," Dick explained. The train had stopped in Chicago near the Pacific Garden Mission, and while the soldiers were helping themselves to coffee and doughnuts, someone at the mission had taken Dick aside and explained the gospel message to him. Dick had listened politely, even with interest, but when the man invited him to accept Christ, Dick's response had been, "No, not now. Not yet."

It was the news of his grandfather's death and Dick's subsequent realization that his grandfather was probably unprepared for eternity that served as a wake-up call. He told me that a few days before, right after he had gotten into town, he'd gone to the pastor of the church where we attended youth group and told the pastor that he wanted to be baptized.

"I was feeling really guilty. And shaken." Dick shook his head. "I went to Reverend Beadles and I explained everything that had happened, and he told me that he would baptize me this Sunday at church. So this morning, when I was ready to be baptized during the service, the pastor said, 'Dick Corley, will you here and now accept Jesus Christ as your personal Savior?'"

Dick turned to stare me in the face. "And I realized I was missing something," he explained, his voice softening. "So right after the service I went across the street to the park and prayed to receive Christ." Dick glanced at me. "What do you think about that, Doreen?"

His narrative had given me enough time to gather my thoughts. "I think that's wonderful," I told him, smiling.

Dick furrowed a brow. "But. . .Doreen. . .are you saved?" His tone was gentle, but the question nevertheless cut deeply.

"Yes, I am." I answered promptly, wanting to avoid any conflict, and Dick, though perhaps skeptical, was appeased for the time. That night, however, as I lay in bed, his words replayed on loop in my mind. *Doreen, are you saved?* I refused to answer, even to myself. I had certainly had enough exposure to the gospel to be able to articulate it clearly; but did that make me 'saved'?

I spent the rest of the summer and the next semester adjusting to Dick's life changes—as a passionate person who committed wholeheartedly to every path he chose, Dick took his conversion very seriously. His first step, just a few weeks into his conversion, was to be re-baptized.

"Dick, is that really necessary?" I asked him when he told me. One baptism was respectable; two seemed like overkill.

"It is." Dick was unwavering. "Baptism is for believers, and when I was baptized the first time, I wasn't a believer. Now that I've been saved, I have to do it if I'm going to be obedient."

I didn't argue, for the topic of salvation was dangerous territory. I didn't really want to scrutinize the state of my soul too closely, let alone let Dick do it for me.

Dick was also invested in fervently praying about his future, and he soon became convinced that the Lord was calling him to do something special. Knowing that the Presbyterian college he attended was not training him adequately for the life in ministry toward which he was headed, he decided to transfer to a different school for the upcoming spring semester.

Long Distance Romance

In January, Dick moved about 30 miles away from Decatur to enroll in

Lincoln Christian College. His finances were tight, and he ended up living in a mortuary to cut costs (naturally). During that time, much to both our surprise, he was offered a position pastoring a small church close to Decatur, which allowed me to see him more frequently (though this was by no means certain—Dick often had to hitchhike back and forth to services). The semester flew by, and at the end of it, Dick sat me down for yet another serious talk.

"Doreen, I think I'm going to transfer to Moody Bible College."

"Where is that?" I could only think in terms of distance.

"In Chicago." Dick watched me closely, monitoring my reaction.

"Why?" I wanted to object, but I knew enough of Dick's determination to realize that he was unlikely to change his mind.

"Lincoln teaches that you have to be baptized to be saved."

"Is that such a big deal? You've already been baptized twice, so you fit the bill and then some, right?" While I didn't necessarily believe the doctrine, I wasn't sure that it was worth losing Dick to Chicago for it.

"Doreen, that's everything. That's why I was baptized a second time—Jesus saved me, not baptism, and if you take the work of Christ out of my life, I lose the only thing worth living for." My own sense of guilt and uncertainty regarding spiritual 'stuff' once again served as a gag against any further argument.

So it was decided; that September, Dick moved north to study in Chicago. Despite my misgivings, I found that our long distance relationship thrived. Thanks to the weekend passes he obtained courtesy of his father's job with the railroad, Dick was able to continue pastoring the church in the area, and I was therefore guaranteed to see him at least once a week. Each Saturday the two of us would go visiting among his parishioners, and following Dick's Sunday morning services, we were able to have the afternoon to ourselves before Dick had to travel back to Chicago. Each Sunday when he climbed aboard the train back to Moody, Dick would begin a letter to me, and we wrote faithfully nearly every day that we were separated.

We were the best of friends; ironically, the only issue on which we disagreed was also the most important. Dick was still unconvinced that I was actually a Christian. I wasn't entirely sure, myself, but my years in church had granted me enough knowledge regarding salvation to be inoculated to truth. Dick was not heavy-handed in addressing my salvation, but he was persistent, and I became increasingly uncomfortable as he gently continued to push me to confront my spiritual life. I was willing to go with him to Youth for Christ every Saturday night, but was starting to feel awkward in the meetings as I attended under Dick's watchful eye and the power of my own increasing convictions.

A Life-Changing Experience

One Friday night, shortly after Dick had arrived in town, he mentioned a Jewish evangelist who would be speaking at a local church that night. I agreed to attend the meeting, though I had secretly been hoping we could just go into town to get a hamburger that night.

My hamburger cravings increased ten-fold once we reached the meeting and I realized what I was up against. The evangelist who was speaking that night was powerful; the truths he spoke somehow slipped through the cracks of my denial, and I had to fight just to keep myself from walking out of the room outright, let alone to maintain a sense of composure.

When the speaker made the altar call I felt compelled to move to the front, but one glance at Dick kept me firmly in my seat. *I already told him that I'm a Christian*, I remembered. *In fact, I've fought with him about it. I can't go up there now. He'll think I'm a liar.* Dick caught my gaze and leaned in with a look of concern. "Are you ok?"

I managed a weak smile, but as he turned back to continue listening to the speaker, I had to wrestle my emotions back with a will of iron. *You need to tell him*, some part of me insisted, but the thought of losing him intercepted the confession on the tip of my tongue. As soon as the meeting was over, I begged Dick to take me home.

"I thought you wanted to get a hamburger," he said, offering me his arm as we turned back toward my house. "It isn't too late."

"I think I need to lie down," was the only honest answer I could muster, and brushing off his worries, I all but dragged him back to my house. I hurried to bed, where I spent a sleepless night arguing with myself over whether or not to admit to Dick (let alone myself) that I wasn't a Christian—and whether I even wanted to be a Christian. After all, I had made it that far without any sort of commitment.

The next night was Saturday, and Dick and I went on our usual date to Youth for Christ with Don, Pat and our friend Irma in tow. I managed to stay composed until we walked in and I saw the speaker. It was the same evangelist who had spoken at the meeting the night before. I managed a begrudging smile at God's sense of humor before bracing myself for yet another tough meeting. I was relieved that the hall was full, so Dick and I had to separate from the rest of the group and find seats far in the back, where I felt free from prying eyes.

The message was once again powerful and convicting, and when we stood at the end to sing "I Surrender All" during the altar call, I choked on the words. I stood, trying to hold back the tears as the music cascaded around me. I knew exactly what I needed to do, but fear and pride were compelling chains, keeping me locked in place.

Dick turned to me and saw my barely-contained tears. Leaning over, he whispered in my ear, "If you want to go up front, I'll go with you."

My tears unleashed in response to his gentle understanding, and I could only nod in response. Slipping from my seat, I walked slowly down the aisle, grateful that Dick was following closely behind.

"Pat?" I saw my sister and Don kneeling up the front, Irma beside them, and I moved to place a hand on Pat's shoulder. She glanced up and we shared a smile through our tears as I sank down next to her.

"Um. . ." I knew how to pray in theory, but this felt more real than anything I'd done before. *"Um. . .God, will you. . ."* I had to take a breath, but Dick squeezed my shoulder and I pressed on. *"God, I know I'm a sinner. And*

I know that you're the only One who can take that away. Will you please? I really am willing to surrender everything. Whatever it takes."

It was February 5, 1950 when the simple act of total repentance and surrender forever changed my life trajectory.

". . .If You Marry Me. . ."

"Dear Doreen,

I pulled my cardigan more tightly against the brisk late September breeze and settled myself on the front steps to peruse Dick's latest letter. He had headed up to Moody for the fall semester, and the separation was particularly difficult following the enjoyable summer we had just spent together.

". . .and if you marry me, you'll have to think about living overseas."

I jolted back from my reminiscences to re-read the sentence. The words were not wholly unexpected. Ever since his salvation, Dick had been eager to go on the mission field. While most boys his age were pursuing college educations or stable blue-collar careers, all Dick wanted to do was proclaim the gospel. I should have been prepared for this bold confrontation. While the knowledge that Dick's passion had huge implications for my future had been in the periphery of my mind for many months, this was the first time the details had been made explicit.

It only took about 3 seconds for my growing passions for both Christ and Dick to direct me. That night, I seated myself at my desk and wrote with calm certainty, *Dick, wherever you go, I'll go.*

It was the beginning of a life I had never anticipated.

Dick and I were engaged shortly thereafter and we made plans to marry the following summer. Dick would have to transfer to a different school if we followed the plan, for Moody did not allow married students to be enrolled unless the couple had been married for at least 6 months; Dick was adamant that he wanted to get married as soon as possible; ergo, shortly after our wedding day on June 30, 1951 we bought a 28-foot trailer, hooked it to our car, and drove from Illinois to Tennessee, where Dick would continue his seminary studies at Tennessee Temple University.

The conditions were crude; the trailer we had been able to afford had no bathroom, and it was what I could only assume would be a character-building experience to have to traverse the length of our trailer park every time we needed the facilities.

"Doreen!" One week a few months after school had begun Dick threw open our front door, excitement radiating from him.

"What is it?" I peeked through the doorway of the kitchen to take a good look at my husband's face.

"Today they started a missions conference at school." Dick strolled into the kitchen and perched on the nowhere-near-big-enough kitchen counter, earning himself a dirty look. "You need to come tomorrow and see it; I've never seen so many missionaries in one place!"

I smacked his leg until he finally consented to slip off the counter. "I can come tomorrow."

"Good." Dick said. He leaned over to snitch a bite of the dinner I was preparing. "Today there was a speaker talking about India. There are millions and millions of people there who have never heard the gospel—Doreen, what do you think about India?"

"I-India?" I couldn't say that I had ever given it much thought at all, but something in me sank at the thought. Rather than argue, I decided to gather specifics. "When?" I asked. "And what about the baby?" While the unexpected pregnancy had not changed our resolve regarding missions, it would certainly have to be taken into account before we moved to a new place.

Dick patted my stomach with a smile. "Don't worry about the baby," he assured me. "God will take care of us wherever we go. And it won't be for quite some time, anyway," he said, half to himself. "Getting approved to join a mission and going through candidate school takes quite a bit of time."

As Dick turned and skipped the two steps back to the living room to begin his homework, I could only pray. *Lord, please not India. I know I said I would go wherever Dick goes, and I will. I promised, and I'll stick with that. But Lord,* I informed Him, *India would not be my first choice.* While I had nothing against India as a culture, while, in fact, I *knew* nothing about India as a culture, the visions of snake charmers that plagued my brain over the next several weeks kept me wary of Dick's new plan of action.

Dick, on the other hand, was haunted by the statistics the missionary speaker had shared regarding the millions of Indian people who had no witness, no human channel to the Savior, and as a man of action, he wanted to take immediate steps toward solving this problem. Within a few short days, his excitement had begun to ignite mine, and by the end of the month, we had written to a mission board called International Mission, Inc. to see if we could get the preliminary papers and start the process of heading to India.

Their response was prompt. Dick hovered over my shoulder as I tore open the envelope and began to read aloud,

"Dear Mr. and Mrs. Corley, (I had to suppress the little shiver of joy that still ran down my spine when I saw the name 'Mrs. Corley')

Thank you for your interest in joining India Mission and going to India with our company.

Unfortunately, the situation in India right now is somewhat volatile, and it is very difficult to get Americans in as missionaries. (I shared a wink with God).

The field in Pakistan, however, right next to India, is also largely unreached.

Would you be willing to consider going to Pakistan with us, instead?

I stopped reading and looked up at Dick, eyes wide. "Pakistan?" I walked to the other side of the living room and picked up our tiny globe, spinning it until I located Pakistan.

"Well, what do you think?" Dick glanced at the globe momentarily before leaning back and crossing his arms to scrutinize my expression. "I know you weren't that thrilled with India—but what do you think about

Pakistan?"

I took a deep breath as a faint trace of guilt at my reluctance worked its way through me. *I will not make this more difficult than it already will be*, I suddenly resolved. "Pakistan sounds wonderful," I said, working my way into a smile. "Let's try it."

That night we sent our response in return: "We would be happy to consider Pakistan." Our nightly prayers regarding India suddenly revolved around Pakistan, and I felt the Holy Spirit working to grant me the ability to be willing and grateful to go wherever we were called.

The going, however, was slow, and our focus soon changed from a mentality of hurry to one of preparation. Stevie's birth, for one, necessitated a change of pace. I developed horrific toxemia-induced swelling eight months into the pregnancy, and during what I thought was a routine check-up, the doctor ordered that I be admitted into the hospital immediately. After a stressful week during which I turned into some kind of human balloon, the doctors frantically tried to keep my blood pressure and swelling down and Dick nearly went off his head with worry, the doctors finally induced early labor, and on March 11, 1952, Stevie came into the world.

Dick and I were caught off guard by the demands of life with a newborn. Stevie was colicky nearly every night from the day he came home from the hospital, and after two weeks of trying in vain to soothe his constant fussing I took him back to the doctor, desperate for some sort of relief from my sleep deprivation, feelings of helplessness, and the suspicion that I might be a bad mother.

The doctor smiled reassuringly at me. "Don't worry, this will pass soon enough," he promised. "But in the meantime, let me give you something to help soothe Stevie." He offered me two medicines. "Try the one in the red bottle first," he advised. "Then, if that doesn't work, use the medicine in the green bottle the next night. That'll definitely knock him out."

That night, I gave Stevie the medicine from the red bottle. I took the green myself; I figured I needed the sleep more than he did.

Several months after Stevie's birth, I took advantage of my spousal discount at the university and began taking a hodgepodge of classes to prepare myself for wherever we would end up on the mission field. Dick was extremely busy, getting up early for classes in the morning only to head from there to his work as a carpenter's assistant. Despite his hard work, however, we found ourselves struggling to make ends meet.

Provision

As Dick walked in from work one evening, fatigue etched into the lines of his face, my heart sank. I had hoped to talk to him about grocery money, but he was clearly exhausted. There was no way I could deepen that wound. I dished up the last bit of ham bone we had and spooned over it the gravy I had made with the last of our flour. *Well, Lord, I'm just a modern widow at Zarephath now*, I prayed. *You provided so well for her--please provide for us as well.* I was not too concerned with Dick or myself missing a meal, but I really hated that Stevie might have to go hungry.

Dick slumped in his chair and looked down at his plate, furrowing his brow. "Is there anything else to eat?" he asked, his face peaked.

I tried to compose myself before meeting his gaze. "That's all for today," I said. "Please remind the Lord tonight in your prayers that we'll need some breakfast tomorrow."

He bit his lip. "I will." The defeat on his face made me want to cry. I sat at the table and lay one hand on top of his.

"God promised that he would take care of us," I reminded my husband. "We're doing our best to follow him faithfully, so he'll work out the details."

Dick squelched the frustration that flitted briefly across his face. "You're right," he said, taking a deep breath and cutting into his ham. "And this is delicious," he smiled, squeezing my hand. "I don't know how you manage to make a delicious meal out of absolutely nothing, Doreen, but it's going to be a very useful skill in Pakistan!"

I smiled and leaned over to kiss his forehead. "Thank you, dear." I bent lower and whispered, "I'm so proud of you, honey." I knew he worked himself to the brink of exhaustion to provide for us.

Dick glanced down at his plate and blinked hard as he took another bite of ham. I squeezed his shoulder, then stood to give him some space. "I'm going to go read for a bit," I told him, moving toward the living room. As I entered, I glanced at the floor by the door and did a double take.

"Dick! Did you have a dollar in your pocket when you came in?"

"No." Dick tracked every dollar within an inch of its life. "Why?" He appeared in the doorway, wiping his mouth with a napkin.

"Oh my word! Honey!" I bent down to snatch up the dollar bill that lay beneath the mail slot. "Dick, someone pushed a dollar bill through our mail slot! How did they. . .?" Any further thoughts were subverted by the relief and excitement that washed over me, and I plopped onto our worn sofa, staring at the Lord's tangible provision in my hand. This would easily buy us enough staple groceries to get us through the next few days.

"Well, you prayed, didn't you?" Dick walked over to me and took the bill from me, staring at it as though he was scared it would suddenly disintegrate. He grinned as we made eye contact, then sat down and threw his arm around my shoulders, bowing his head. "Thank you, Lord," he prayed, relief filling the cracks in his voice. "We know you've promised to provide; thank you for always fulfilling your promises. Thank you for being trustworthy and faithful. We love you."

I added my fervent "amen" to his prayer.

God's provision throughout the next several years continued to astound us. One morning I answered a knock at the door to find myself face-to-face with an unknown man holding two large bags of groceries.

"Hello," he said with a grin. "I was told to bring this to you."

I stared at him, puzzled. "Are you sure?" I asked him. Stevie and I had finished the last bit of food in the house that morning, but I had not yet told Dick. Besides, even if he had wanted to send us food, there was no way he had money to buy even a bag of rice, let alone two full bags of groceries. We had just gone over the budget the night before.

"I'm sure." Despite the man's confidence, I resisted his attempts to hand me the bags. I didn't want to mistakenly take someone else's groceries.

"I don't think so," I told him, uncertain how to proceed. "We don't have any money to pay--"

"This belongs to you, ma'am." The man moved past me through the house, setting the bags on the kitchen table.

"Thank you." I gave up trying to understand the situation and decided to simply enjoy it. "God bless you, sir."

The man touched the brim of his hat with one finger and walked out the door, while I collapsed into a chair. *Lord, what have You done!?!* I could not hold back my laughter. *How do You do it? Thank you, thank you. . .* I stood and unpacked the groceries, more excited to prepare lunch than I had been in months.

Dick shook his head in awe when I told him about it later that evening. "Doreen, God wants us on the mission field," he said as I finished the story. "Look at how he is preparing us to trust him!"

"And to live off of nothing, like real missionaries!" I laughed. "He's certainly doing something," I said, moving to the sink to wash the dishes. I felt a rush of gratitude as I ran water over the dirty plates—they symbolized that God had provided us with food yet again.

Loss and Heartache

Finances were not our only difficulty.

Dick and I discovered in the spring of 1953 that I was pregnant with our second child, due in December of the same year. Having always wanted a big family, I was incredibly excited at the thought of having a second child, but there were early danger signals. I started to experience perpetual bleeding, which the doctor attributed to a tearing placenta. In order to minimize damage I was put on strict orders to avoid stairs and rest often. It was hard to follow those orders, especially with an active one-year-old, but I was determined to do everything I could to save the little life inside me.

Unfortunately, nothing could be done. I was admitted to the hospital on my birthday, two months before the due date, and my second little boy arrived unable to breathe and pronounced stillborn. It was my first major experience of loss—but it would be far from my last.

Four days after our second baby's anticipated due date, Dick and I were startled from our beds by a violent pounding on our door. I followed behind Dick as he stumbled to answer it. A policeman was standing on our doorstep, holding a piece of paper. "I'm sorry to bother you, sir," he said, "but you need to call this number. There's been a death."

Peeping over Dick's shoulder, I gasped when I realized that the paper listed my family's number. "Dick. Oh, no." I was awash with cold dread.

"Honey, why don't you go to the pay phone and call? I'll be right behind you with Stevie." Dick grabbed my coat and helped me pull it on, pulling me into a brief hug. I stumbled numbly across the park to the community pay phone.

Who could it be? Mom? Dad? Surely not Jackie or Pat. I could not fathom that any of my immediate family members could be gone; but I had a horrible sense of dread as I thought about either of my parents passing. While my sisters had each made professions of faith, my parents remained, if not callous, at least uninterested.

I picked up the phone and slipped in the change Dick had given me, trying to calm my shaking enough to dial. "Mom?" I blurted the moment I heard the receiver on the other end pick up.

"Doreen?" It was my mother's voice, and I breathed a sigh of relief. *She's ok.* Maybe the death was one of my extended family members. But my mom cut all such hope short with her next breath. "Honey, it's Dad."

"Dad?" I leaned against the pay phone for support; my entire body felt suddenly weak. *Dad? Not my young dad. He's only 49! He's healthy! And young!*

And—"

"Honey, he had a--" My mom's voice broke. "The. . .the doctors said he had a cerebral hemorrhage. He was fine tonight, just his usual self, but then he stood up, and. . ." My mom choked up again.

The remaining conversation was brief; stunned into numbness, I had little to contribute. My mind played back to a scene two short weeks before.

"Dick, I think I'm going to write my dad a letter," I mused aloud over dinner.

"Ok." Dick had the bemused look of a man who has not yet quite picked up on his wife's need to verbally process her thoughts.

"I wouldn't normally," I explained. "Dad's not much of a letter-writer, or letter-reader for that matter. But I really feel like I need to write to him, maybe to explain the gospel."

"Ok." Dick said again.

*It was all the encouragement I needed. That night, I sat down and wrote my father the most pointed letter of my life, ending with the challenge: ". . . .*Dad, your girls will be in heaven. Will you be there with them?"

"Doreen?" I blinked back to the present to find Dick standing beside me

"It's Dad." My throat closed.

"Oh, honey." Dick wrapped his arms around me gently.

I felt as though I had been thrust into an unwanted crucible of faith. I had to trust that God was not inflicting the pain cruelly, and that He would sustain me through it. We managed to take a weekend off of our busy schedules, and rushed to be by my mother's side. It was a blessing to be able to comfort my mother; we would not have been able to travel that far on such short notice had our second child been born on his anticipated due date. While it certainly didn't "make up" for the loss of the child, I was able to come to something of a better understanding of God's timing in the whole process.

The funeral weekend passed in a blur. As we drove home late that Sunday night, I leaned my head against the seat and blinked back tears as pain washed over me anew. *God, this hurts so much.* I didn't know what else to say.

In that moment, the words of a song we had sung at youth group suddenly came to mind:

Does Jesus care when I've said "goodbye"

To the dearest on earth to me,

And my sad heart aches till it nearly breaks—

Is it aught to Him? Does He see?

Oh, yes, He cares, I know He cares,

His heart is touched with my grief;

When the days are weary, the long nights dreary,

I know my Savior cares.

That song would carry me through grief time and time again.

Iran? Where's That?

The trip to the mission field, in the meantime, continued to be somewhat up in the air. Dick and I prayed daily that God would guide us to wherever He would have us go, all the while tentatively preparing for Pakistan. While it would be years before we were able to go, in the meantime I wanted to find out as much as I could about this mysterious place across the globe.

To make ends meet we had taken the position of house parents at nearby Zion College, a traditionally African-American school; the free housing and food granted us some financial relief while Dick finished seminary, and I enjoyed getting to cook and care for the girls in our charge.

One afternoon, as I prepared a big pot of soup for dinner, Dick barged into the kitchen and leaned one hip against the counter as he studied me intently, waiting for an opening. My curiosity got the better of my urge to ignore him to see how long it took him to explode with his news. I grinned at him. "Ok, honey, spill it."

"Well, Doreen, we had a missionary speaker in chapel today," he started.

"Was he any good?" I took an experimental sip of soup and then reached for the salt.

"No, he was rather dull."

At this unexpected plot twist, I turned toward him, salt shaker still poised over the soup. "What?"

"Well, he wasn't the best," Dick, ever honest, repeated. "But he's on furlough from Iran right now, and he...well, as he was speaking, I felt the Spirit touch my heart, somehow, and Doreen, I think we should go to Iran unless the Lord closes that door," he finished in a rush.

Iran? Where is that? My knowledge of India and Pakistan had been hard-earned. I knew nothing about Iran. "Oh," was all I felt qualified to say.

"What do you think?" Dick studied my face anxiously.

"Well Dick, I don't know," I said. "I don't know anything about Iran, but you know that I said I would go wherever you go."

"Well, I invited the speaker to dinner tonight, so you can ask him any questions you have then," Dick told me.

I grinned wryly at him. Leave it to Dick to bring home an unexpected dinner guest, then deliver news so big that feeding everyone was the least of my concerns. "Well, I'm glad we're having soup," I told him, too amused to be annoyed. "If you take care of getting Stevie up from his nap, I might even be able to make a salad or something to make the food go further."

Dick headed toward Stevie's room, and I was left to finish the soup and contemplate Iran. *All right, Lord,* I told him. *You know about Iran, you know the needs there. . .I have no idea, but if we can do good there, then I am willing to go.* I rejoiced at the speed with which I was able to surrender—God had clearly been working in my heart during the last several years.

Our meeting with Mr. McAnlis, the missionary speaker, was eye-opening. He told us about the orphanage at which he worked in Iran; he told us of the of 56,000-plus villages in Iran without a witness; he told us about the desperate need in Iran for knowledge of a Savior.

As soon as he left, I curled up in a corner on the couch to ponder everything I'd just heard.

"Well?" Dick sat across from me, watching my expression closely.

"The needs there are almost overwhelming," I told him, then grinned. "But surely—in a country with almost no missionaries—surely there we can tell *someone* about Jesus."

Dick smiled. "I was hoping you would be interested."

Once we set our faces toward that country we never looked back, and all our preparations focused in that one direction. Dick completed his third degree, while I decided to pick and choose classes that I thought would be useful on the field, and in addition to my responsibilities with Stevie and house parenting, classes such as storytelling and flannel graph painting consumed my time.

The process was relatively swift this time around and by June of 1955, we were on our way to candidate school. There we saw Allen McAnlis again and met his wife Harriett and their two young children, Kathy and Jim. The evaluation process was quick but thorough, and on July 9th, we received our acceptance letter. From there, I felt as though we had been thrust into a wrinkle in time, of sorts; everything we did focused on November, when we were to set sail. Support-raising, packing, getting immunizations (so many immunizations!), saying goodbyes--all our frenzied activities melded together into a jumbled memory mosaic.

And so it was that in early December, 1955, I found myself at the house of a family I'd never met in a city I had never before seen, surrounded by a people I did not know and a language I could not understand.

4 Village Life

"Mama!"

Jolted from my memories, I turned to see Steve standing behind me. It took a concentrated effort to remember where we were. *Oh, right. The hospital in Kermanshah. We got here last night.* I glanced at the bed across the room where Dick was still snoring softly.

"Mama!" Stevie crawled into my lap, shaking my shoulder to get my attention. "Mama, I'm hungwy!"

I hugged him close and gave him a kiss as his irresistible little boy smell filled my senses. "Good morning, honey!"

"We pway cars?" Stevie was not about to let his new surroundings or even his hunger distract him from the truly important elements of life.

"Sure, honey," I said, heaving myself to my feet. "But we need to get you ready for the day first." After our forced bathing drought over the past several weeks of travel, I was eager to take full advantage of the tub while we had it, and Steve was rudely diverted from his desire to play cars by the thorough cleansing process he had to undergo at my eager hands.

Even though Dick and I could have slept for days, we were too excited to get up and explore to sleep in very much, and we were awake, clean, and relatively functional by late morning; the afternoon passed swiftly as Dr. Bussdicker showed us around the hospital and compound. Our excitement-fueled energy was quickly depleted, though, and by the time we settled in for an early dinner, all three of us were ready to go back to sleep. I declined tea in hopes of an early bedtime.

It was not to be. Just as we finished dinner, we heard a commotion in the yard and hurried to the window to investigate. A familiar figure lept from a dilapidated jeep and strode toward the door.

"Allen McAnlis!" Dick hurried out to greet the guest, with Stevie and I close upon his heels.

"Hello hello!" Allen grinned. "I came into town for supplies today and heard that the Americans had finally made it, so I came to pick you up and take you back to the orphanage! Are you ready for the last stage of your journey?" He smiled sympathetically as Dick and I nodded in sync. It was almost surreal to be so close to our destination after so many weeks.

From the City to the Village

We loaded up the jeep, and as dusk swept the land Dick and I crawled into the front seat to begin the final leg of our journey. Though we would eventually be headed to the city of Hamadan for language study, we were going to spend several months working at the orphanage with the McAnlises and the Heydenburks, local missionaries, while we made living arrangements in Hamadan. As the Jeep took off into the night, I could only hope that this would be the first and last time I would ever have to ride a Jeep over unpaved, unlit roads. Every time the vehicle hit a rut, I was in danger of concussing myself on the roof, and the headlights were more than inadequate to pierce the thick blackness that hung over the land. *I'll bet the stars out here are beautiful, though*, I told myself, trying to look on the bright side. It was only moderately encouraging.

A din kicked up in the distance, and I cocked my head, attempting to decipher any familiar sounds. "What is that, Allen?"

"Oh, it's the village dogs," he explained. "Every time we go through a village, their watchdogs come out. In fact, you should always send word if you're going to stop in a village at night, so that the people can lock up their dogs until you've arrived."

"Oh." I didn't particularly care for watchdogs, and the near-deafening racket informed me that I would feel no special endearment toward the Iranian variety.

As the Jeep drew closer to the barking, I glanced outside and saw a huge shape looming against the blackness. I gripped the door handle in one hand and Dick's arm in the other, silently directing his attention to our assailant. He patted my knee and leaned over me to get a better glimpse of the dog. . .no, now there were two. The Jeep suddenly seemed very small, indeed.

The two Iranians hitching a ride in the backseat chatted and laughed with one another, apparently unconcerned with the instruments of destruction hovering outside their windows. I tried to take my cue from them, leaning back and breathing deeply against terror. I seemed to be getting a lot of practice in combating terror of late.

"Doreen, you're cutting off my circulation," Dick whispered in my ear, and I realized I was gripping his arm in both my hands.

"Have you *seen* those animals?" I whispered back, unapologetic. "If they're going to get me, you're coming too."

"Don't worry, they can't get to you." Allen had apparently overheard us. He patted his dashboard affectionately. "This jeep has been pitted against much worse."

I barely contained my skeptical snort.

"In case I haven't made it clear enough, I am so glad you both are finally here," Allen continued, his soothing voice obviously trying to calm his passengers as much as impart information.

"I'm sorry we weren't able to send any word," Dick said. "It was late when we got in, and--"

"Please don't worry about it." Allen interrupted with an airy wave of his hand. "It was no inconvenience to bring you back today. And I even bought hot dogs before I knew you all were in town!"

"Oh, please don't worry about that," I hastened to console him in my turn. "We're used to anything—we ate on a student budget for four and a half years!"

I couldn't identify the muffled sound (a snort of laughter, perhaps?) that came from the driver's side, but I had an inkling that I had made a faux pas.

"What did I do?" I murmured close to Dick's ear, and he shrugged. We would later learn that hot dogs were a rare and very expensive treat in this part of the world. My response to Allen's gesture of hospitality would become a running joke at the orphanage for years to come.

We had left the watchdogs behind by that point, but I quickly found that letting my guard down was a foolish move. The number of villages between Faraman and Kermanshah were legion, and each of them seemed to be populated with an identical mob of vicious, flesh-eating creatures out for blood. I could only hope that the orphanage was not similarly populated, for if such were the case, I would feel no shame in refusing to budge from the Jeep until morning.

Arrival

When we finally pulled into Faraman, I breathed a sigh of relief—we seemed, for the time at least, to be safe. When the gatekeeper slid open the big iron doors to let the Jeep into the yard, I peeked out to ensure that the guard dogs had stopped safely outside the walls of the compound before I slid out of the car, stumbling a little on my stiff legs, and squinted in a vain effort to get my eyes accustomed to the dark. There were only a few tiny blips of light fighting off the darkness around us.

"What are those lights?" I asked Allen, pointing. They were too bright to be candles, but certainly not effective enough to be electric.

"They're Primus lamps," Allen said, straightening his lanky frame from where he was helping the gatekeeper unload the jeep.

"Uh. . .what?"

"Pressure lights," Allen explained. "They're fueled by kerosene, and you have to pump them to keep them on."

This was unexpected. I loved electricity. I was familiar with candles. Pump lights flirted with the edge of absurdity. I sighed—yet another thing to adjust to. Would it never end? Something told me probably not.

"All right, come with me, folks." Allen grabbed a bag and headed toward one conglomeration of lights. Dick and I followed obediently, clinging to our worldly goods and staring about us in a bewildered fog.

"Harriett!" Allen loped up to one of the houses and shoved the door open with his foot. "I brought a surprise!"

"Yes, Allen, what is it?"

"The Corleys are here!" Allen placed his bundle down and gestured for us to enter the house.

I squeezed past Allen into a small tiled hallway to meet the gaze of a gracious brown-haired woman who beamed a welcome upon me.

"Oh, hello Doreen!" She enfolded me in a warm hug, and I fought back tears. Finally, after a month of travel, I felt a tiny stirring of 'home'.

"It is so nice to see you again," Harriett continued, reaching around me to extend a solemn hand to Stevie. "We've been expecting you for days! And how are you young man? You seem to be getting handsomer every day, you know that?"

"Yes." Stevie smiled winningly. He had quickly learned that being the only blonde boy within a thousand-mile-radius came with a slew of benefits.

Harriett laughed. "And you know it, too, don't you? Come in, come in!" She pinched Stevie's cheek, then straightened to oversee the process of exchanging our shoes for house slippers. "Iranians don't wear their outdoor shoes in the house," she explained. "No doubt you've heard of the famous Persian carpets? They go to a good deal of trouble to take care of them."

The examples of carpeting I saw in the hallway alone were well worth protecting—beautiful designs flourished around the borders of the colorful works of art.

"Please, you must be starving," Harriett said, leading the way to the dining room, where a table was set for the four McAnlises.

"Oh, I am so sorry," I said, abashed. I hadn't realized what time it was. "I know you weren't expecting guests, and we don't need to eat--"

"Psh! All the way from Kermanshah, and not eat?" Harriett brushed aside my worries. "We've already decided that you'll be eating most of your meals with us, anyway. If you would just put bowls on the table for the three of you, we'll have dinner on in a jiffy," she promised, and in a few short minutes we were pulled up to the table, enjoying a simple but hearty lentil soup complete with thick slices of homemade bread.

Allen kept up an effortless flow of conversation, and I was thankful that he was willing to carry the bulk of it, for I barely made it through half a bowl of soup before my eyes began to register the sand-filled feeling of sleep deprivation. The spoon felt increasingly heavy in my hand, and I felt my eyelids slowly sink.

Clink!

My head jerked as my spoon made hard contact with the bowl. "Oh dear, I'm sorry," I exclaimed, trying to pull myself back from the brink of sleep.

"Oh my dear, you must be exhausted!" Harriett exclaimed, looking from Dick's face to mine. Stevie was already passed out; mercifully, he had missed his soup bowl on the way down. I could barely muster a nod.

"Allen, why don't we take them over to the Heydenburk's right now." Harriett stood to clear the bowls. "Oh my dear!" She suddenly stopped and stared at her husband. "Allen, we forgot to tell the Heydenburks that the Corleys are here! Honey, why don't you run right over there and tell them," she continued. "I'll help them put on their coats and shoes and walk them over right behind you. Doreen," she addressed me, bustling about, "they'll have a bed ready for you by the time we get over there."

She was right. It took just a few moments to maneuver our heavy limbs into our coats and cross the compound to where the Heydenburk's house stood. Introductions barely registered, and I only had time to shake Clem's hand, hug Alpha, and wave at their three daughters before Alpha bundled us off to the back room that would be home for the next few months.

The room was large and quite cold, but the bed was piled high with several layers of blankets, and a few moments of concentrated shivering under them warmed the bed to a comfortable level.

I can't believe we're here! A jolt of excitement shot through me as I drifted to sleep. *I wonder what tomorrow will hold?*

Exploring Faraman Village

The Heydenburks, bless them, allowed us to sleep in and for the first time in weeks, I woke up feeling both refreshed and settled. I stretched and poked Dick with one chilly toe. "Wake up, Dick! We're here!" Dick flipped over to face me, barely propping one eye open.

"I know, honey," he mumbled, drifting back to sleep. I grinned as I debated pushing the issue, but mercy prevailed.

I hopped out of bed and dressed quickly, leaving Dick to finish sleeping in peace. Stevie popped up soon after he heard me stirring, and I dressed him, too. "You're going to meet a lot of new children today," I informed him as I pulled on his little shoes.

"What childwen?" Stevie wanted to know.

"The orphanage children," I told him. "There are lots of children here whose parents can't take care of them. So the McAnlises and Heydenburks take care of them."

"How many?" Stevie was slightly wary at this prospect.

"Oh, I would say about 40 or so."

"FORTY?" Stevie's eyes grew rounder. 40 new playmates! He didn't look as though he was entirely sure how he felt about that, and I ruffled his hair with a comforting hand. "You'll like them.'

He looked unconvinced, and I decided that experience might be the best teacher in this instance. "Come on, sweetie," I told him. "Let's go see them."

Stevie grabbed my hand, then looked up at me with a furrowed brow. "I want bweakfast," he announced, and I laughed. New playmates were clearly not his immediate concern.

"Like father like son, eh? Ok, honey, let's go find the kitchen." We wandered out of our room and made our way to the kitchen through the house's single long hallway.

"Good morning!" Alpha turned from the sink, where she was washing the dishes. "Are you all hungry for breakfast?"

Stevie and I nodded in tandem, and within short order we were devouring the traditional breakfast with which we were by now familiar: fresh loaves of flatbread, tantalizingly salty feta cheese, home-churned butter, and Alpha's grape jam. A delicious sort of cracked wheat porridge was also served, along with the expected cups of tea.

Clem appeared in the doorway as I picked up a lump of sugar and slipped it between my two front teeth. "Picking up the customs already, I see!" he laughed delightedly, and I smiled in triumph. The first time I had seen someone sip his tea through a sugar cube, I had been fascinated and a little appalled; but after the multiple cups of tea with which we had been plied by hospitable Middle Easterners, I had finally managed to pick up the custom without (I hoped) looking completely ridiculous.

"It's good to see you putting in so much effort to drink tea properly," Alpha said with a smile. "It means a lot to people when you take the time to learn and appreciate their customs."

"Especially tea drinking, apparently." I shook my head in amazement. "Allen told us to be prepared to drink tea, but I had no idea! I do love it," I hastened to add. "It's just that there's so *much* of it."

Alpha laughed sympathetically. "Tea is a part of every major event in most, if not all, Middle Eastern countries," she agreed. "And Iran is no exception."

"And how's the little man?" Clem swept in to give Stevie a sticky high-five. "You want to come and meet the other kids?"

Food had given Stevie courage, and he readily assented to being wiped off and taken to explore the "Big Room," where the orphans had classes and ate their meals. "We'll give you and Dick a tour as soon as he's awake," Clem promised as he lumbered from the room, Stevie giggling from his shoulders.

"Do you need anything to settle in?" Alpha asked as she took a seat by me and poured herself a cup of tea. "Well, you probably don't even know at this point," she answered herself. "But please don't hesitate to ask for anything that you do need!"

"Thank you so much." I took another soothing sip of tea. "I'm just glad to have a place where I can feel settled for a little while."

"It is a draining trip, isn't it?" Alpha sighed. "I'm always exhausted after it, and I've done it enough to know what to expect. It's much harder when you're headed into the unknown."

I nodded. "But it's exciting, too," I pointed out. "We've been praying and hoping for this for so long—I'm just glad it's finally here! I can't wait to start learning Farsi and getting to know the kids!"

"Ah, the energy of youth!" The older woman smiled at me. "I'm so glad you two were willing to come," she added. "I know you must be sacrificing a lot."

I felt myself flushing. "Well, it's been what we've wanted to do ever since we were saved," I explained; then, trying to change the topic, I added, "Tell me more about the orphanage."

Alpha was happy to talk about the place where she and Clem had invested so many years of their lives. She explained that the orphanage had been founded by Dr. Francis Stead, a Presbyterian missionary who had originally come to Iran to do medical work. As he traveled from village to village, he became disturbed by the huge number of orphans he noticed. Because the mission that supported him did not do orphanage work, he eventually left that ministry in order to buy the land where Faraman was currently located and develop it into a village of sorts, hiring farmers from the surrounding villages to work the land. Clem and Alpha had joined the ministry over 20 years ago.

"Most of the orphans are children whose mothers died in childbirth," Alpha explained. "The fathers usually have too many children at that point to be able to take on the extra burden of a newborn."

"Wow. I can't imagine," I murmured.

"Can't imagine what?" Dick ambled through the doorway, planting a kiss on my head before sitting down to pour some tea. "Where is Clem?"

"He's probably at the Big Room for lunch right now," Alpha said. "Speaking of which, we should probably join him. Doreen, I talked your ear off this morning!"

"Not at all," I reassured her.

"We have a cook who makes meals for the orphans, and we try to eat with them as often as we can. So we'll go to our main room for lunch today," Alpha explained, standing.

Alpha directed me to bundle up, and I was glad I had—despite the compound's thick walls, the wind sweeping through the courtyard cut sharply against any exposed sin.

The Big Room was set against the far back wall of the compound, behind the McAnlis's house, which stood in the center. The Heydenburk's house was against the far right wall of the compound, so we found ourselves cutting a diagonal path across the courtyard to walk behind the McAnlis's house and reach the Big Room.

We entered in a rush of cold wind, and I felt suddenly shy as 46 pairs of eyes fixated on me. Two long strips of cloth, running the length of the room, served as 'tables', with children sitting cross-legged on rugs next to them. I saw Stevie, one blonde head in a sea of dark ones, chattering away with another little boy; I was glad to see he had overcome some of his natural shyness. It probably helped that he had no idea that his new little friend couldn't understand a word he was saying.

I walked with Alpha to the head of the room, where a few girls who looked to be about 9 or 10 were sitting. They watched every step we took, giggling and averting their eyes whenever I glanced in their direction. Alpha asked them something in Farsi, gesturing to the empty spaces by them at the *sofreh*. The answer was apparently in the affirmative, and I seated myself next to a beautiful dark-eyed girl named Farideh. Alpha conversed easily with the girls in Farsi, and I felt a yearning to do the same; *soon*, I tried to reassure myself, knowing that language lessons were just around the corner. For the moment, I stuck to communicating through smiles and head nods. At least I was fluent in body language and charades.

As Alpha and I made our way back to her house after leaving the children to complete their lessons, I sighed with contentment. It may just have been the influence of getting to interact with the precious children, or even the delicious meal (rice and dates with flatbread), but I felt that I could learn to love this place.

The First Christmas

We had arrived at the orphanage on the 13th of December, and the next several days flew by as Dick and I began to get used to the rhythm of the orphanage, worked to coordinate trips to Hamadan to search for a house, and attempted to free our freight from Beirut, where it was being held hostage by the shipping company's Middle Eastern sense of time. It wasn't until December 23rd, as I sat at the typewriter to work on the latest draft of the "Corley Courier," our newsletter, that I realized our dilemma.

I typed the date on the page and felt a mental jolt. "Dick, tomorrow is Christmas Eve!" I spun around to look at him.

"What?" Dick looked up at me. "I totally forgot about Christmas!"

Without the commercial trappings of Christmas, the decorated trees, the holly and red bows and music surrounding us, we had completely forgotten the season.

"What do we do?" I asked. "I didn't even think about Christmas when I packed. I didn't put anything in there for Stevie."

Dick pondered for a moment. "Well, maybe he won't notice if we just package up some of his Tinker toys," he offered with a mischievous smile.

I could only muster a half-smile. "Seriously, honey, what are we going to do?"

Dick was also stumped, and we decided to go to Allen and Harriett with our troubles. Since arriving at Faraman we had been eating most of our meals at their house, and had adopted them as our mentors.

Unfortunately, this time the news they shared was disheartening.

"We don't really do much for Christmas," Harriett informed me. She shook her head sympathetically as my face fell. "Sometimes we have American soldiers come in," she said. "They'll bring little things like apples and oranges for the children; or missionaries will bring in missionary barrels they were sent earlier in the year, so the kids will get new hand-me-downs and stuff."

"Is there even a Christmas tree?" I was trying to be gracious, but my disappointment was poignant. Even though Dick and I had lived most of our lives in near-poverty, we had always been able to go somewhere—a friend's house, a department store, *somewhere*—to get our annual dose of Christmas beauty and cheer.

"No, we don't tend to do a Christmas tree." Harriett said gently. "We'll read the Christmas story with the kids, and you and Dick and Stevie are welcome to join us for that."

I agreed, disappointed but appreciative Harriett's sweet spirit.

Dick managed to hitch a ride into town the day before Christmas to pick up some small plastic toys for Stevie; it was a valiant but disheartening effort.

When Christmas morning arrived I was still struggling to shake my sense of disappointment. We read the Christmas story, but there was no special Christmas coffee cake for breakfast, no presents, no tree, not even a single sprig of holly. It took all my willpower and a good deal of prayer to plaster a smile on my face as we finished the Christmas story before walking down to the Big Room for lunch. While I had never thought I enjoyed the more commercial side of a traditional American Christmas, I was yearning for a taste of something familiar after months of feeling culturally off-balance, and Christmas had seemed like a perfect time to reset myself to a state of emotional equilibrium. *Maybe they'll have a little something special for lunch*, I thought, trying to cheer myself up.

In the Big Room, a few American soldiers who had joined us for the day were interspersed among the children, creating enjoyable chaos. The children were gleeful in light of the attention and fresh fruit the soldiers gave them, and I almost felt a tinge of Christmas spirit myself when I plopped to the floor by some of the girls with whom I had become acquainted.

"Sakineh made a special meal today," Harriett informed us, sitting down next to me.

"What is it?" I asked eagerly.

"Ghorme-saabzee."

The little girls on either side of me clapped their hands at the news.

"Come again?" I barely refrained from saying a tart *Gesundheit*. I didn't know what this mysterious dish was, but something told me it didn't involve turkey or cranberry sauce.

"It's the unofficial celebration dish of Iran; it's that good," Harriett told me. That was all I knew as I walked through the line to get my bowl. The cook had made a huge pot of rice, over which she was pouring a green sauce flecked with meat, beans, and onions. There were many adjectives I could have used to describe it, but I would never have accused it of looking appetizing. My heart sank. *All I want is a little bit of Christmas,* I thought as I followed the girls back to our seat on the floor. *Nothing special. Just a piece of holly tied with a red bow.*

As I approached my seat I saw Fanus and Nasreen, two of the girls, eating their food with massive smiles. They were unaffected by unmet expectations. They had no idea what Christmas was "supposed" to be like. *I will not be outdone by the good attitude of an 8 year old*, I thought to myself. *Doreen, you absolutely* must *have a good attitude!* Having thus made up my mind, I soon found that following through on my resolution was not as difficult as I had anticipated. The *ghorme-saabzee* turned out to be delicious, and the girls' sweet spirits kept me from being able to dwell too much on my 'sorrows.'

After dinner Dick and I headed back to the Heydenburk's house, where I ended our Christmas doing yet another load of laundry by hand. Our freight (and my little hand-operated washing machine) had not yet arrived, and I resigned myself to the idea of doing laundry by hand the rest of my life. "Dick, when do you think our freight will get here?" I asked him as I scrubbed at one of Stevie's perpetually dusty shirts. Our boy had made fast friends at the orphanage, and I didn't see him all that often, as he spent the better part of every day with the little boys his age. Judging from the amount of dirt he was able to accrue each day, he was having a grand time.

Dick shrugged. "It should be any time now," he said.

"That's what they keep saying, but we could have made the trip ourselves twice now," I complained. Dick agreed, but there was nothing we could do. Neither of us had anticipated the pace of the culture in which we now lived. Several days later we got word that our freight had shipped on December 26th, over three weeks after we had arrived in Beirut. Harriett McAnlis was sympathetic, if slightly amused by my distress.

"Well, dear, it's just the way we do things here," she told me as I helped her prepare lunch. "Iranians have a very different perspective of time than Americans. Over here, things get done when they get done."

I shook my head, barely able to comprehend the situation. "I just don't understand why they would hold onto it for so long," I told her. "Isn't it more of a hassle to find room to hold all the freight than it would be to just ship it?"

Harriett shrugged. "I wish I could explain it," she said with an encouraging pat on my shoulder. "But you'll learn that there are certain cultural norms here, or in any culture, really, that defy explanation."

"It's not a huge deal," I replied, perhaps more for my benefit than for her. "I'm just tired of washing our set of clothes every other day. But," I brightened, "at least the freight has been shipped, so it should be here anytime, right?"

Harriett smiled at me and refrained from replying. She was well aware that it would probably be weeks before our freight was delivered.

Despite these slight hiccups in our plans, our time in Faraman passed happily enough; yet throughout it all, we eagerly looked forward to moving to Hamadan.

5 On to Hamadan!

In an effort to get us to Hamadan as quickly and smoothly as possible, Dick and Mr. McAnlis made a few overnight forays to that city in search of housing for us while we continued to wait for our freight. Though I hated being separated from Dick while in still-alien surroundings, the thought of settling into our own home at last made me hustle him out the door each time.

In the meantime, I felt that I was soaking in more knowledge of

Iranian culture and language by the minute. Dick and I had begun preliminary language lessons with a man who lived near the compound, Mr. Mirzai. We spoke comparable amounts (ie: none) of each other's respective language, and it was quite a shock to my mental system to try to understand his Farsi. The language did not sound as guttural as the Arabic I had heard in Lebanon and Iraq, but I still found it difficult to distinguish between the sounds. Our sessions progressed thus: Mr. Mirzai would say a word and I would repeat it, inevitably missing some nuance of tongue or inflection. Mr. Mirzai would repeat the word back to me, attempting to emphasize whatever slight sound it was I had omitted; and for the next five minutes we would say the word at each other with increasing levels of frustration on both sides until Mr. Mirzai was satisfied. By that point in the exercise, I was never entirely sure what it was that I had done correctly, but was simply eager to move to the next word.

Pronunciation was not my only language worry; vocabulary lacked the logical flow I expected. One day, having learned that the word for door was *daar*, I was eager to decipher the word *daaryaw*, and spent several minutes trying to pry from my teacher what the word *yaw* meant, figuring that putting the two smaller words together would help me deduce the full word. When he finally discovered what it was I was trying to do, Mr. Mirzai simply shook his head. "No, no!" he exclaimed, and managed to indicate that *daaryaw* meant ocean.

"Oh, well that makes sense," I griped to myself as I eyed the word in disgust. "If *daar* means door, then naturally, the next word that has the word *daar* in it should mean ocean!"

Mr. Mirzai was very patient.

As another element of cultural immersion, I put aside my watch and joined the villagers in using the sun as my timekeeper. "Come to church when the sun is behind that building!" were typical directions—not that any such instructions mattered. Many people would show up to the service as we sang the closing hymn, and that was after we started a few hours later than advertised. It drove my time-oriented self crazy.

While I was enjoying each day at the orphanage, I found myself still craving my own home, and praying hard that the freight would arrive so we could move.

The City of Queen Esther

Finally on one cold February day, the long-anticipated freight arrived, and we could proceed with our move to join the Burrises, the missionaries located in Hamadan. We had learned that Queen Esther and Mordecai were buried in that city and I could hardly wait to explore it.

Our goodbyes to our dear friends in Faraman were casual, for we knew we would return to live at the orphanage following our language study. The older children were harder to say goodbye to, for we had no reason to expect that they would still be there in two years.

But we were finally on our way! The drive was arduous; normally a 3 hour endeavor, it stretched to 9 with the trailer we had to add for our extra luggage. The jeep we had commandeered for the trip was hardly adequate. To make matters worse, there wasn't a single restroom between the cities.

We arrived with a storm that night, and after drinking the mandated cup of tea with Omer and Harriet Burris, I tumbled into bed, almost too excited to sleep. *Tomorrow I'll have a home!*

The next morning Dick and I left Stevie with the Burrises so that we could explore our new city.

"I'm so excited to see our house!" I could barely refrain from skipping with glee.

"Yes, I—" Whatever Dick was about to say was squelched in a yelp when a shovelful of snow tumbled onto his head and down his shirt collar.

"Dick! Are you ok?" I couldn't help but laugh as I brushed off the snow to reveal Dick's disgruntled expression.

"I'm fine." Dick leapt out of the way as another clump of snow fell by his side. "What is happening?!"

I looked up in time to dodge my own snow assault. "I have no idea. We can ask the Burrises when we get back and dry you off."

We turned on our heels and headed back to the Burris's house, where they explained to us that the rooftops in Hamadan tended to be built flat rather than sloped; after a snowfall, therefore, people would scurry to their rooftops to shovel the snow to the streets below before it leaked into their homes.

"Never look down while walking in Hamadan during the wintertime," Harriet Burris laughed when we told her our tale.

"Lesson learned," Dick assured her. (We should have listened better. Not 3 weeks later, we would show up at the Burris's door begging for extra containers to capture the melting snow that was leaking through our roof all over our apartment.)

Thus equipped with essential tips for survival, Dick and I sallied forth again that afternoon to inspect the house he had chosen for us.

He had done exceedingly well. The two-story house included a large walled-in backyard with grapevines and almond and cherry trees. I couldn't imagine how beautiful it would look in the springtime!

Dick had already warned me that an Iranian family occupied the downstairs portion of the house; they would be moving within the next few months to make room for Joel and Sara Slaughter, a young couple who would be joining us in our language studies. We opened the door and hurried up the steps, hoping not to disturb our new neighbors.

The floors in the house were all brick, and I wondered how, exactly, one cleaned a brick floor as we toured the house. The three bedrooms, living room, and dining room all passed inspection, but I paused on the threshold of what Dick told me was the kitchen.

"This is the kitchen?" It looked exactly like every other room in the house. Dick had warned me that the house was not quite up to par with the high standards I had developed in our trailer home, but my mind had pictured the kitchen as more than just an empty room. In my optimism, I had even been imagining that there would be a faucet or two.

"Well, it's what I figured we could use as the kitchen." Dick shrugged. "It's above the kitchen in the apartment downstairs, so it just seemed to make sense, though I guess it really doesn't matter that much."

"Ok." I took a deep breath and reminded myself to be grateful. At least we had thought far enough ahead to bring along such appliances as a refrigerator, stove, and oven, all kerosene-operated.

We finished the tour of the house without incident, but one oversight made me anxious. "Honey, where is the bathroom?"

"It's...downstairs." Dick smiled at me, chagrined. "In the Iranian family's apartment."

"*In* their apartment?" This was an unexpected blow. I only hoped that family was prepared for us to use their facilities, because I certainly did not know enough Farsi to explain if I was caught sneaking around their home.

Between the sparse kitchen and the unfortunately located bathroom, my brain was spinning as we made our way back to the Burrises house.

Lord, can I live like this? I asked him, my eyes welling up with tears. *Without even running water in the kitchen? At least we had running water in our trailer.*

Doreen, do You trust me?

Lord, I—I paused. Did I trust Him? He had granted me salvation, a wonderful husband and child. He had allowed us to raise enough money to get to Iran, had protected us in the storm over the Atlantic...this house somehow fit perfectly into His provision for us. *Yes, Lord.* I decided. *I do trust You.*

That conscious shift helped lighten my mood, but my head was still whirling when we arrived back at the Burrises.

"Did you like it all right?" Harriet winked at me when she caught sight of my face and I felt somewhat comforted. She must have experienced my exact sentiments just a few months before.

"It's—" I searched my brain for an appropriate adjective. "It's overwhelming, for sure."

Harriet nodded and reached over and hugged me. "You may not

believe this now, but I promise it will get better," she said. "And Omer and I are here if you need anything. Truly."

I smiled gratefully at her. I hoped I wouldn't take advantage of that invitation beyond all reasonable proportions, but suspected that hope was in vain.

A Crash Course in Missionary Life

Over the next few days Dick and I scrambled to buy bed frames and other necessities. Because Hamadan is one of the coldest places in Iran, we also bought a pair of portable kerosene heaters, and immediately received an impromptu kerosene lesson.

The first night in our new home, we sat in the dining room, eating our dinner while one of our heaters went to work making the living room a bearable temperature. "Honey, would you turn up the temperature?" I asked Dick, fighting off a shiver. "Maybe we could get the heat to reach in here?" He headed to the living room.

"Honey, switch the light on!" I called after him. Fiddling with a kerosene wick in the dark seemed a surefire recipe for disaster.

"It *is* on!" Dick called back. I couldn't see anything in the palpable blackness emanating from the doorway. Curious, I ran to the living room; darkness covered the surface of the room. The kerosene heater had gotten a little overambitious, and in addition to heat was giving off smoke and soot that coated the walls and the light bulb in a layer several inches thick.

I steadied myself against the doorframe. "Oh. . .no." I choked on the soot-filled air.

Dick wrapped an arm around me. "I'm sorry, honey. We must have turned the wick up too high."

We were too defeated to laugh and too tired to be angry. I did the only thing I could think to do. "Let's go to bed," I suggested. The last few months had trained me to expect that things would look brighter in the morning, and I clung to that lesson.

Sure enough, when I woke up the next morning, I found that things were brighter in a metaphorical sense, though strictly speaking the living room was still blanketed in grime.

I sent Dick to the Burrises house to borrow cleaning cloths and a bucket, and Harriett returned with him to help us scrub down the living room and assure us that this was a common occurrence among people who had never used kerosene before. Though the job took most of the morning the oil paint on the walls made it relatively simple. I wondered if the builders had anticipated some such incident.

February 1956

Dear Mom,

We've finally settled in at Hamadan. Well, I use the term 'settled in' somewhat lightly—our stuff is in a house, but whether or not we have a roof over our heads is less certain! Just two days after we moved in, we had our own personal rainstorm, courtesy of a lethal combination of rain and poorly constructed roof. Thankfully, it did provide us with plenty of fresh water, so that the man we've hired to carry water to us every morning had an easier time of it for a few days.

Mom, I wish you could see our kitchen! When we arrived, it was just a room, no faucet or anything. It could have been a bedroom. Like I said, we had to hire a man to drag in water each day. The little stove we brought along tries hard, but the kerosene here is so incredibly dirty that it's hard to keep anything clean. And when it comes to baking, we can only set our little oven over two of the stove burners and hope for the best. Last night I was baking some biscuits, and when I opened the oven door—Mom, would you be willing to send us some scouring pads? The poor biscuits were completely soot-saturated and. . .well, I had to double-check my recipe book just to remember what they once were. I'll never take scouring powder for granted again! There's no bleach or anything sold here, so once things are grungy, they're grungy for life. I hope this doesn't sound too negative. Our house has beautiful fruit trees in the back and lovely brick floors—and it's so spacious! The Lord has been good to us!

I must be off now—it's time to make dinner. If you are *able to send those scouring pads, would you also please include a Ball book on canning? I think I'll need to begin canning next summer. The markets are pretty sparse here in the winter, so we need to find a way to preserve some produce.*

Sorry, this letter has been all about us! It's hard to adjust to everything being so new all the time, but that's no excuse—how are you?

All right, must be off. Give my love to Jackie and Pat and Don.

Love,

Doreen

Language study was the first priority on our agenda, and within days of our arrival in Hamadan, Dick and I had met and hired Zahra and Muhammad Mesbah to teach us Farsi. The couple had worked with missionaries through the Presbyterian mission before our arrival, and their advice and training regarding Iranian language and customs proved invaluable to us. Zahra was a patient perfectionist, and she refused to let me get by with anything less than flawless communication abilities. Dick and I were determined to beat language study at its own game, as it were, and committed to a steady diet of 6 hours of language study a day, for at least 5 days of the week.

```
                              Khisban Bou Ali


                              Hamadan, Iran

                                 August,
                                    1956

Dear Friends,

   It has been a few months since we put
together our last prayer letter; thankfully, and
thanks largely to your prayers, life here is
progressing more or less smoothly.

   Dick and I reached the 3-month mark in our
language study and passed our exams, only to find
```

out right afterward that we were expected back at the orphanage immediately to teach Vacation Bible School for two weeks. We quickly put aside our regular curriculum and focused on putting together lessons, in addition to learning how to *teach* those lessons! Then, right after we got there, Dick came down with hepatitis, so his role during the course of the week was to stay in bed sucking hard candy and turning yellow. Thankfully, Mr. Mirzai, an Iranian evangelist who works at the orphanage (you may remember that he was my first language teacher), was able to step up. His name means 'God's helper,' and he certainly was during those two weeks. The VBS went well, I presume, though I don't really know Farsi for 'constructive criticism', so I may have gotten some of that which I overlooked. We had to stay at Faraman an extra week for Dick to recover, and it was so nice to finally get back on a bus to take the long trip back to Hamadan.

It's still surprising sometimes to discover how poorly one language translates to another. For example, when I made a cake for Steve's birthday several months ago, it fell badly. Zahra was baffled when I tried to explain it to her using the word "fall". So I finally got up and showed her the cake, and she instantly understood. "Oh," she said, "the cake slept!" That was not at all the meaning I was intending, but apparently it conveys the proper meaning to Iranians.

Dick and I are also getting a chance to see language study from the other perspective, as a few neighbors have hired us to teach them English. Please pray that through this means, we can share the gospel.

We so appreciate your prayers as we continue to settle in. Pray that our language study would be diligent and fruitful. Praise God for our wonderful teachers!

"FOR WE PREACH NOT OURSELVES, BUT CHRIST JESUS AS LORD: AND OURSELVES YOUR SERVANTS FOR JESUS' SAKE." II Corinthians 4:5 "BRETHREN, PRAY FOR US."

Your servants,

Dick and Doreen Corley

While my language study came mainly in the form of Zahra's instruction, Dick's Farsi was improving daily thanks to his frequent interactions with shopkeepers as he sought to make the house more livable. His ingenuity knew no bounds.

"Honey, if I had known you were this useful, I would have married you a few years earlier," I told him one day as I perched on the window ledge watching him drill a hole in our kitchen floor. He had arranged that the local tinsmith make a large funnel to insert into hole so that I could drain water from our floor into the kitchen sink of the apartment below us. It was not a perfect arrangement, and took some watchfulness on my part lest I empty my dirty dishwater onto my downstairs neighbor's freshly washed vegetables; but it was still vastly preferable to having to walk downstairs each time I needed to empty our sink bucket.

Eating Out

"Meesus Khorlee," Faraj said in halting English, as he pulled his shoes on to go home after a language lesson, "You and Meester Khorlee . . . come eat. . .wiz my family?"

"Faraj, that was very good," I exclaimed. "Dick and I would love to eat with your family! When?"

Faraj looked at the ceiling, trying to find the right word. "Two days?" He held up two fingers, just to be sure.

"You'd like Dick and me to come eat with you in two days?" I clarified, nodding. "That will be Wednesday."

"Ah, yes. *Wednesday*." Faraj stumbled a little over the word. "I. . ." he made a walking motion with his fingers. "Take you."

"You'll come pick us up?"

He nodded again. "I come pick us up."

I bit back a smile and decided to let it slide. We were only a few lessons in, and poor Faraj was already overwhelmed with all that he was learning.

"All right, Faraj. Thank you. I'll see you in two days," I said.

He ducked his head slightly and turned to walk home.

I shut the door, my head awhirl. This was it; our first time really experiencing famous Persian hospitality. I had no clue what to expect.

"Nervous?" Dick murmured two days later as the three of us followed Faraj down the street.

"I've been trying to think of conversation topics ever since he invited us," I said. "But I can only say about three sentences about each thing, so I'll be lucky if I have thirty minutes worth of conversation. Let's hope they're very interested in the price of oranges and the location of the restroom."

"Well, I can talk to them about pretty much anything involving home maintenance," Dick grinned. "And I bet they've always secretly wanted to know the process of having a sink funnel built."

"Of course." I sighed. "But they do this often enough . . . surely they must have *some* conversation starters ready."

"Yes, they probably do. In Farsi. Just like we have some conversation starters in English. It'll be fine," Dick added as worry crept into my expression. "It's our first time out. It's bound to be uncomfortable. But it won't kill us. At worst," he joked, "everyone in the neighborhood will just avoid the weird foreigners."

And with that comforting thought, we arrived at the house.

Every sense was on high alert as we climbed the steps of the apartment building and walked down a narrow, concrete hallway to Faraj's door.

He entered the apartment and stepped aside, ushering us into the foyer. Dick and I mimicked his every move like marionettes, removing our shoes when he did, placing them in the corner, and following him into the sitting room. The room was ringed with chairs, tiny tables sitting between every pair. There were a few men, presumably Faraj's family members, already seated.

Dick and I were directed to a couch on the far end of the room, and getting there required that we run a social gauntlet. Faraj introduced us to each person; Dick greeted each one with a traditional kiss on both cheeks, while I offered them my hand.

Was that right? Was I supposed to shake hands? Nod? I knew instinctively not to exchange kisses, but beyond that, proper etiquette eluded me. They each grasped my hand politely, though, and if they were offended, they covered it beautifully.

We finally reached the couch and had a moment to take in our surroundings. The room was beautifully decorated, with thick Persian carpets lining the floor. A table in the center of the room was piled to breaking point with plates of cakes and cookies, platters of fruit, and little bowls of nuts.

Are we supposed to go up to the table and get the food? I wondered. As the only woman, my role seemed doubly obscure. *Am I supposed to serve it to everyone?*

I was thankful to see Faraj take charge of the situation. He walked up to the big table, filled two little plates with thin slices of cake and a few cookies, and brought them to Dick and me. As he did so, an older woman wearing a head covering stepped into the room.

"My mother," Faraj said, glancing at me for the stamp of approval on his English.

I nodded encouragingly at him and stood to kiss his mother on both cheeks. She nodded to Dick, poured our tea, and quitted the room.

Am I supposed to follow her? Help her in the kitchen? Everything was so new and bewildering. *Why didn't I ask Zahra about all this? I don't even know what questions to ask until I suddenly need the answers!* This seemed to be a common theme in this collision of cultures.

Since I didn't know what to do, I felt that it would be best to take the path that required the least explanation, and I plunked down next to Dick and Stevie and tried to help Dick carry on the conversation.

It was slow going. Our hosts' English and our Farsi were similarly lacking. After the first halting attempts at conversation, we were at risk of falling into silence altogether. Faraj was solicitous in his hospitality, constantly coming to fill our plates with something else; fresh cucumbers, which he demonstrated we were to peel and coat in salt and pepper; delicate, crumbly cookies; tea cake, etc. His mother, whose name I could not remember for my life, came in to pour a second round of tea. Casting my eye about the room for a point of conversational interest, I noted the ornately carved salt and pepper shaker set Faraj had placed on the table in front of me.

Girding my Farsiac loins, I dove in. Catching her eye and pointing to the set, I told my hostess, "What beautiful. . .things." I felt the power of my compliment deflate under the weight of my crude Farsi.

My hostess, though, seemed to be overwhelmed with gratitude at my lame attempt at a compliment. She burst into a string of excited talk at me, while I smiled and nodded along, eager to encourage whatever positive feelings might be blossoming between us.

Faraj rushed to her side to translate. "You. . .take," he said, putting the shakers into my hand.

"Take?" I glanced from one to the other, hoping I was misunderstanding.

Faraj said something in Farsi, and I caught the word "keep."

"I think it's a gift, Doreen," Dick was also closely watching our hosts.

Horror filled me as I realized my mistake. "Oh!" I slammed the shakers back on the table in my eagerness to be rid of them. "Oh no no no!" I said, rapidly shaking my head. "Faraj, I couldn't take them," I blurted, then realized I was speaking in English. Switching to Farsi, I gave my refusal a good old college try. "Thank you," I managed, "But I. . .no." It was the best I could do.

The mother kept insisting, I kept refusing, Faraj kept trying to translate for both of us, and Stevie finally saved the day when he reached over to get a cookie off my plate, burned his finger on my hot tea glass, and sent up a wail.

My hostess rushed to get some cool water for him, while I cradled my little man in my lap and promised myself to not admire anything about the house the rest of the night.

We sat. And sat. And sat. The Iranians talked and laughed among themselves, always checking on us and trying to engage us in the conversation whenever possible, but the language barrier hung between us like a veritable gag order.

I was starting to feel a migraine blossoming at the base of my neck. I needed something more substantial to eat if I was going to make it through the rest of the evening, but nothing seemed forthcoming, though my plate was never emptied of cookies and cucumbers. Dick noted my distressed face and asked Faraj politely when people ate dinner 'in your country'.

Faraj shrugged. "We'll eat when my father comes home."

"And when will that be?" Dick kept his voice casual, as though he was just gleaning interesting information.

Faraj shrugged again. "Anytime, I guess."

Anytime sounded positive. I dug through my purse for some aspirin, but I hadn't brought any along. Stevie had been sitting quietly next me, coloring in a book that I'd brought along for him, but he was starting to get restless, and I could tell we were bordering on tantrum territory. It was already eight thirty, and the poor boy was used to going to bed at around this time.

Please come home, I mentally begged Faraj's father as I bent over Steve, offering him cookies and rubbing his back. "It's all right, honey," I told him in a low voice. "We'll get to eat soon."

I'd never lied to my child before, and I wasn't aware I was doing it then, but "soon" dragged into "Here Stevie, have another cookie," dragged into a muttered, "Dick. . .should we just go?" dragged into *Lord God, if You don't do something miraculous, I'm going to be sick on this beautiful carpet.*

Stevie was huddled in my lap in a heap of half-asleep misery by the time we heard the front door open.

Thank you Lord! I tensed my muscles, prepared to haul the whole party to the dining room. The father came in, was introduced, and then. . .sat down. And picked up a small plate, which he filled with cake and cookies.

"What. Is. Happening?" I hissed into Dick's ear, gritting my teeth against the pain in my head.

"He has to get appetizers too, I guess." Dick said.

I sagged against the couch in defeat. That was it. I was taking the Migraine Express all the way to Misery City.

Dick patted my shoulder. "You just sit," he told me. "I'll handle this." He turned to our host and began to make conversation, complimenting things that the man couldn't give him (ie: Faraj's work ethic, the house as a whole—although I wasn't too sure we were going to get away without a generous real estate offer if Dick didn't tone down his enthusiasm over it) and discussing aspects of Iranian politics that Dick had learned from his frequent contact with shop owners.

I sat gazing off in a migraine-induced stupor, focusing my limited energy on details like keeping my mouth from hanging open and my eyes from falling closed. Stevie seemed to sense that this was not the time to start fussing, and cuddled quietly up to me.

Just as I leaned forward to tell Dick that I "absolutely have to go home right now", Faraj's father stood and invited us into the dining room for food. Food! The word jolted hope into my aching brain as we followed him to the dining room. The table was laden with food. I hurried to take my chair, bowed my head, and waited for the prayer. The clink of dishes brought me back to myself, and I glanced up to see Faraj staring at me.

"Are you all right?"

I flushed. "Yes, yes," I assured him. "I'm fine."

Dick was grinning at me a little more widely than strictly necessary as he spooned a thick meat sauce over the rice Faraj had spooned onto my plate. "You'll feel better after you eat, honey."

I could only hope. Sitting there listening with one ear to the conversation Dick was trying to carry on with our host, coaxing a crabby-to-the-brink-of-meltdown Stevie to eat something, and trying to soothe my own aching head was one of the most miserable moments in recent memory. I felt terrible for poor Faraj, who kept glancing at me in concern, and all I could offer him was a tight-lipped smile of reassurance.

Conversation at the table was belabored, and after 15 minutes of forced effort, Dick finally gave up and focused on the food. The silence was a blessing. I focused on getting one forkful of food after another into my mouth. It was slow going, but finally we were all finished. *We can go!* I stood up with the most enthusiasm I had mustered all night.

Alas, the night was still young in the minds of our hosts. Dick and I were ushered back into the sitting room, where the appetizer table had been replenished. A little bowl of nuts and plates of cake were placed in front of us, and the conversation picked up and took on a life of its own as we chattered and ate still more food. Stevie was nearly apoplectic in his exhaustion at this point.

Dick took a look at my face and finally said, "All right, dear." Standing, he told Faraj how much we'd appreciated being invited over for dinner. They pressed us to stay, but Dick refused. "Thank you so much, but I think we really must go." Since he couldn't yet explain a migraine in Farsi, he just repeated the sentence until Faraj put his shoes on and walked us home.

I crawled into bed that night feeling like the first ever missionary failure. "How bad was that?" I asked as Dick walked into the room. He sat on the bed and patted my shoulder.

"Go to sleep, honey."

I groaned. "It was that bad?"

Dick shrugged. "It was a rough night for all of us, love. Don't worry about it. Go to sleep for now, and we'll talk about it in the morning."

"Fine." I flipped over and started drifting to sleep as Dick changed and crawled into bed next to me. ". . .Dick?"

"Hm?"

"Did you see how much food she had to make? I don't think I've ever made that much food at one time, even at the college."

"Well, honey, you can always practice on me. I won't complain." Dick leaned in to kiss me.

"What a martyr you are," I laughed as he rolled over to sleep.

September, 1956

Dear Mom,

How are you all? I haven't heard from you in awhile, and would love to know what's going on! Of course, as slowly as the postal service goes between here and Illinois, there are probably two letters on their way already, in which case, thank you for your letters.

We finally feel settled into Hamadan, thanks largely to our wonderful new helper/handywoman. I don't really know what to call her, since she kind of does everything. Maybe 'right hand' would be the best title, considering! Her name is Tubah, and she came to us from the orphanage. I bonded with her during our stay there, and since she is 14, and a little too old for the orphanage at this point, the McAnlises asked her if she'd like to join the hapless new foreigners in Hamadan. I'm not sure how that sales pitch was successful, but oh, what a help she is!!!

I thought that I was a reasonably contented person until I met her. She's used to life not giving her exactly what she wants. She works hard, and is not remotely put off by the slight obstacles we encounter every day, such as trying to boil water on our kerosene stovetop, with the wicks located several inches beneath the pot and the burners designed too closely together to allow for more than one pot to sit on the stovetop at once! One of her main jobs is heating the water for us to drink and prepare tea with—it takes forever, and I am becoming convinced that I would not be able to survive here in Iran without Tubah's help! She has not once complained about using our tiny, hand-operated washing machine, or even about the fact that she has to use the restroom—or the hole in the floor masquerading as a restroom!—in a stranger's apartment. She's also just started a round of sewing classes, with the result that she's practicing by sewing us new clothes! I can't tell you how much I appreciate that—it is SO cold here, Mom! None of us have enough warm clothes, so Tubah has been a huge help in that arena, too. She's such a Godsend; I really can't say enough about how much good she's done for us!

She's also been very helpful in our language and culture study. Every night after we've put Stevie to bed, Dick and I settle down with Tubah in the living room, and she tells us a story from her childhood, from local folklore, or just made up out of her head.

Poor thing—it can't be gratifying to have your captive audience mumbling things like, "What? What was that? Can you repeat that word?" or talking to each other: "Honey, did you hear that? Did you understand that?" I suspect that our understanding of Persian folk tales will be horrifying to our neighbors, should that topic ever come up in conversation.

Oh dear, I must be off. I certainly didn't mean to take my entire letter-writing time to expound upon the marvels of Tubah, but I felt that you needed a proper introduction to the newest member of our family!!! We're actually having our first dinner guests tonight! I'm trying not to panic—Tubah has done everything. She told me what to get at the market, and I got it. She showed me how to decorate, and I did it. My social life is in the hands of a 14-year-old. The hazards of missionary work they never warn you about. . . .

Much love,

Doreen

I pulled the letter from our typewriter, typed the addresses onto the envelope, and folded the one into the other. Dick would take it to the post office in the morning. "So Mom should have it by. . .November at the latest. Maybe I should add a note about Thanksgiving." I smirked at that, shaking my head. It would be funnier if it wasn't true; being out of contact with my sweet family was one of the hardest parts of "missionarying."

Stevie wandered in, blocks in hand. "Mommy, will you play with me?" I glanced at the clock. It was 5:30. We'd told the guests to come at six, so we had at least two hours before we were in any danger of company showing up. "Sure, love." I plunked onto the floor next to him, wriggling to find a comfortable spot on the brick. "What would you like to play?"

With the blocks divided between us, we settled in for a game of "build and then demolish the city." We were mid-way through the demolition phase when the smells of some kind of delicious meal wafting into the room reminded me that of the upcoming dinner party. "I'm sorry, honey, but I need to help Tubah. Stay here and be good." Leaving my son to his destructive instincts, I hurried guiltily into the kitchen.

I needn't have worried: Tubah apparently had some combination of Superman and Betty Crocker in her genes. "Just fine," she answered when I asked her how things were going. "The *khoresh bademjan* is almost done." She held out her spoon for me to taste.

"Tubah! That's fantastic!" I peeked into the pot and identified the eggplant and tomatoes I'd purchased the day before. I'd managed to barter the vendor down to half the asking price, and bragged to Dick about it until Tubah laughed at me. "Oh, that's about right. They set the initial price at double what they expect." Dick and I had spent the rest of the night trying not to think about all the weeks we'd been royally ripped off by paying full price.

"What can I do?" I snuck another taste of the *khoresh bademjan* and grabbed my apron.

"We should start to get the appetizers ready." Tubah pointed to the earthen containers packed with all the cookies, tea cakes, and other appetizers we had made over the past several days.

"Ok!" I put together several platters full of the baked goods, a cooling yogurt dish, some fresh vegetables, and fruit and nuts. Even Faraj' mother would have been impressed. Tubah inspected the platters carefully. "Those are for after the meal," she said, pointing to the fruit and nuts.

"All right." I began removing the bowls, but Tubah laid a hand on my arm.

"No no, Mummy Kuchek. They need to be out there with the appetizers. But I just want you to know not to serve them until the end."

"Oh. . .all right. But why is that?"

"It's so you can sit around and talk, but still have things to do with your hands."

"Wow, that's brilliant! I wonder why we don't do that in America?" I pondered aloud. "Tubah, you're a godsend. How do other people learn these things?"

She smiled and blushed slightly. "And then, after you serve the fruit, no more tea."

"What?" I mock fainted against the wall. "No more tea? In Iran? Impossible!"

Tubah laughed and turned back to her work.

"Wait. . .really? No more tea?" She seemed serious, but I couldn't believe it.

"Fruit ends the meal," Tubah said.

"Oh. How come?" I always felt 5 steps behind the learning curve.

Tubah shrugged. "It just does. No one will take tea after they eat fruit."

"Oh. . .ok." I had nothing to add. If the Fars people wanted to punctuate their meals with fruit, far be it from me to protest.

I set up the platters on the table in our sitting room, placed a tea table between each set of chairs, made sure each guest could have a knife with which to cut their cucumbers. . .the minutia to which I had to attend seemed endless. Dick, who had been visiting some of our neighbors, arrived back minutes before the first knock sounded on the door. I raced to answer it, curious to know who would have arrived first. Harriett McAnlis had told me that in Iran the guests arrive in order of importance, and that I shouldn't be surprised if guests asked me who else was coming so they could gauge their time of arrival accordingly. She hadn't given me the key to this pecking order, though, and I was curious to see who would arrive first.

It was our next door neighbor, Haybat. I wondered how she had ended up being the first to arrive. *I wonder where I rank, socially? How late should I show up to parties?* That thought barely had time to register before the floodgates apparently opened and our home quickly filled with people. I hardly had time to sit that evening, as Tubah and I raced back and forth attending to the needs of our guests. Several times I caught Dick's eyes as he beamed at me, and I could tell we shared the same thought: *This is what we came here to do.* To serve, to relate, to love people to Christ. Though I fell into bed exhausted that night, I could only hope this would be one of many such evenings.

In April the family downstairs finally moved out, and I was somewhat embarrassed to admit how relieved I was—while they had been nice enough people, it had been a daily act of humility to trounce downstairs into their apartment to use the facilities, while the language and cultural barriers made it very difficult to joke with the other family about the awkwardness of the set up. I was hoping that Joel and Sara Slaughter would have a sense of humor regarding the odd arrangement.

The Slaughters arrived shortly after our neighbors left, to great rejoicing on both sides. The couple was of the same age and disposition as Dick and myself, and the four of us were fast friends.

"After all," I told Sara one night, "if we can remain friends as I funnel all my dirty water into your sink, we can remain friends through anything!"

To Persia, With Love

Of Toilets and Tubs

The Slaughters' arrival brought more than merely the relief of a cultural oasis, though it was nice to have someone with whom I could speak English when language lessons became grating; upon Sara's arrival, the two of us decided that using the 'Persian version' of our restroom was vastly over-rated, and begged the men to find a way to transform the hole in the floor to something resembling an 'American Standard' version. The men headed off to the tinsmith, where they ordered a custom-made funnel. When it was completed, they drilled a hole into the seat of a chair, arranged the chair neatly over the funnel, and set the entire contraption over the original hole. Considering our previous facilities, Sara and I felt spoiled indeed by the new accommodations.

Pleased with the glowing admiration they earned from us with this venture, the men went on to tackle the problem of a tub. Dick went out to barter a tin tub from the tinsmith (Dick, by this time, was his favorite customer). The tinsmith's idea of a bathtub looked quite a bit like a coffin, and I had to laugh when Dick finally brought it home—there was no question of where to sit, as one end was significantly wider than the other. Dick also brought a wooden stove home with him; on this he placed one of the 55-gallon steel drums that had served as suitcase on our trip from America. He inserted a spout into the drum, set the spout over the tub, and our bathtub was complete. Sara and I were eager to try out the bathtub, and we quickly developed a pecking order for its use; the steel barrel took far too long to fill and heat for each person to be able to take a bath whenever he or she had the inclination, so instead we would have to arrange when we were all planning to take a bath—then we bathed according to rank, cleanest to most dirty.

The first time we tried this went smoothly for about 10 minutes, until I pulled a dripping Stevie out of the tub and faced an unanticipated dilemma. "Dick!? How do we get water out of the tub?"

Dick came running at my summons and stared blankly at the water. "We forgot to insert a drain," he grinned sheepishly.

"Ha!" I barely kept myself from indulging in a full belly laugh. "I wonder what the tinsmith will say to us about that when we go back for something to drain the tub with tomorrow! He already must think we're insane!"

The tinsmith had a fair number of opinions, all but the most complimentary of which he kept to himself.

December 1956

Dear Mom,

Life here continues much as usual—that is to say, everything feels very unusual, all of the time. I suppose you get used to feeling perpetually uncomfortable.

I hope that day comes quickly, although I guess some things are finally starting to feel familiar. I can go on walks without getting lost, we have gotten to know our neighbors at least a little, and I've started to call our little house home.

Language study continues to go well. 30 hours a week of pure learning is exhausting, but Tubah is here to help with Steve and the chores, and I push myself hard every day to finish my allotted 6 hours early so that I can do something I enjoy—playing with Steve, writing to you, making doughnuts if I'm feeling particularly adventursome.

I feel that we are getting quite a good grasp on the language and culture, but I'm realizing that no matter how hard we work, we'll always stand out. The amount of attention we attract just by walking down the street is unreal—anytime I walk past someone I hear whispers and gasps, and know that if I look back at them, they'll be staring at me. Some of the bolder ones are shameless about it. Last week I decided that they looked exactly as foreign to me as I do to them, and when a group of people walked up to the taxi I was in and smashed their noses against the glass (which happens frequently), I pressed my face up on the opposite side of the glass and stared back. I won that round! Sometimes when I'm out with Tubah or Zahra, they'll scold the people who are staring at us: "What's the matter with you? Haven't you ever seen a human being before?" I don't quite have the heart to do that yet. . .but it's absurd to be stared at like a circus animal when you're just going about your daily business. I've started telling myself that they must think that I'm a movie star, and are staring at me to figure out which one I am; that helps ease the awkwardness a bit—in my head, at least.

I don't want to paint an unfair picture of the people here, though. They may be openly curious, but they are also unfailingly kind and welcoming people, and they regard Americans with a high degree of respect. And they are so generous! Mom, I'm learning to compliment very carefully. They would literally offer you the clothes off their back if they think that is what you, as their guest, would like. I pray daily that I will learn to be as hospitable as the Iranians; I haven't a chance but for the grace of God.

A funny story-- a few weeks back, Dick came back laughing from a visit to Hussein, the carpenter who built most of our furniture. During the visit, Hussein took Dick aside and asked, 'Does it take 9 months for a baby to come in America?' Apparently we appear to be some kind of sub-species of human to him. Dick still isn't sure how he kept a straight face through that conversation. Considering the divisions between men and women here, I'm actually just impressed that Hussein figured out that it takes 9 months for an Iranian baby to come!

And speaking of babies—Mom, you'll be thrilled to know that you're going to be a grandmother again! We are due in June. We're all over the moon, and Tubah can't wait to have a baby around! She feels gypped to have missed Stevie's infancy.

I must be off—it's time to make dinner, and I still have to do another hour of language study. Conjugation may be the death of me yet, but whenever I get tired of it, I remind myself what it's like to go to someone's house and not be able to participate in the conversation, and the iron enters my soul. I will learn to speak Farsi like a Persian.

Give my love to Don and Pat, and Jackie. I miss you all very much.

Much love,

Doreen

6 Ins and Outs of Daily Life

In the following weeks I felt myself growing apprehensive about the birth. We'd arranged to travel to the Nemaze hospital in Shiraz for it, as that hospital was better equipped than anything in Hamadan. I had to wonder, though, what 'better equipped' meant in these circumstances.

While the trip involved some of the hiccups inevitable in such a situation (including a birth that occurred so fast the doctor almost didn't arrive in time and an earthquake occurring in the city the day after), David Wayne Corley was born healthy on the 17th of June, 1957. Davy was a sweet-natured, easy baby, which was a huge blessing—I didn't have any of the magical green medicine left over from when Steve was colicky.

Shortly after Davy's birth, my Ball canning book arrived courtesy of my mother, and Sara and I were inundated with failures as we attempted to can produce for winter. Sterilization was little more than a formality on our tiny kerosene stove-tops, and heating everything to the appropriate temperature at the right time was so frazzling that I was ready to hand in my missionary badge after the first few attempts.

"Who knew that it would be the canning that brought me to my knees?" I groaned to Dick one afternoon, staring morosely at a pot of a failed plum jelly. As it turned out, SureJell wasn't optional. "I don't mind learning new languages or using holes in the floor as a restroom, or bathing once a week. . .but canning might just be too much. You know all those missionary biographies we read before coming here?"

Dick nodded, trying to ignore the thick mess I stirred in vain hope of a miraculous jelling.

"I'll bet they could only manage to be so holy because they never had to can anything."

Dick grinned. "I'm sure it still tastes good." He peeked over my shoulder and seemed to hold back a wince. "Well, I'll eat it in any case."

I laughed somewhat bitterly. "Well, you're welcome to as much of it as you'd like. Wait until you see what I can do to tomatoes!"

The summer passed in a blur of language study, attempts at hospitality, and time with my boys. I was even starting to feel somewhat adept at the canning process when my self-confidence received another jolt as Stevie entered the first grade.

I had loved teaching when I had done Sunday school lessons, both in America and in Iran, and looked forward to teaching my own son. Calvert system for home education in hand, I'd carefully prepared lessons, but failed to anticipate the obstacles Stevie's bilingualism erected.

Having had constant interactions with Tubah and two parents deep in language study, Stevie spoke excellent Farsi and passable English; his ability to differentiate between the two, however, was lacking.

"30 days hath September, April, June. . ." I was attempting to teach him the months of the year when our first obstacle became apparent. Stevie stared, disconcerted, as I listed the names of the months in English.

"But, Mommy, what about *Khordad*?"

"Oh, honey. . .that's the Iranian calendar," I tried to explain.

Stevie cocked his head to the side. "But where does it fit?" As far as he was concerned, if two calendars were good, combining them would be even better.

His vocabulary also lagged. "*Sag!*" He cried gleefully at one point as I showed him a picture of a dog.

"That's the Farsi, honey. Do you know the English word?"

Stevie stared at the picture hard; slowly, his eyes began filling with tears. "T-that's not. . .*sag*?"

"It is in Farsi," I told him. "But it's *dog* in English."

School became a daily battle for us. While Stevie was speeding through some of his first grade lessons, the vocabulary ones were prone to daily melt-downs, as he struggled to work effectively with both languages.

I was thankful that language study was going well, despite the extra responsibilities inherent in teaching a first-grader and working with a rapidly growing newborn. Both boys were sweet and laid-back, and between their easy-going personalities and Tubah's help, I found that I was able to more or less keep up with my responsibilities.

A Different Kind of Christmas

Autumn whizzed by, and though we entered the holiday season with substantially lower expectations than we'd had the previous year, nothing could have prepared us for the Christmas celebration we were to have.

"Doreen!"

I jerked awake at Dick's frantic call. "What is it?" Then I, too, could feel the vibrations. The entire house was violently rocking back and forth. I had only been in one earthquake before, a few days after Davy had been born; even as an earthquake novice, I could tell that this one was bad. "Get Davy!" I screamed at Dick as I scrambled out of bed and wobbled toward the door.

"Tubah! Where are you!?" I flung open Stevie's door just in time to see a piece of the ceiling collapse. "Steve!" I raced to his bed. The debris had just missed him. He was wide-eyed, but unhurt. I snatched him up and wheeled around, nearly knocking Tubah off her feet. She was frozen in place, white-faced and trembling.

"We need to get outside!" I screamed over the rumbling. Tubah just stared at me, shaking. I grabbed her with my free hand and gave her a slight shake. "Hurry!" Tubah turned and ran toward the stairs, with me treading on her heels. Dick had made it out the door with Davy moments before us.

Chaos dominated the scene outside. Every person in the neighborhood was present. Shrieks filtered through whatever air space was not already claimed by wailing. Stevie clung to me with both legs and arms, trembling, too frightened to cry. I brushed debris from his hair and attempted to soothe him with a calming monologue that wasn't effective on my own pounding pulse.

It was 5:20 A.M. on December 13th. The earthquake ground to a halt within several minutes, but the effects were far longer-lasting.

We had been basically spared; compared to the myriads of people who lost their lives, and the hundreds more who had lost their homes, our whole team had fared well. Our home was damaged but intact. The wall in Stevie's room was on the verge of collapsing, so he slept in our room for a few days while we repaired it. One of the single girls who worked on our team, whose one-story apartment was safer than our house, took Davy home with her to sleep each night for the next several days until our nerves calmed a bit. Though we had been spared the worst of the damage, every aftershock had us on edge. We took to placing our shoes on the top of the staircase so that we could evacuate at a moment's notice. Our daily prayer meetings were frequently interrupted by the creak of the building shifting beneath us. None of us wanted to admit our fears (we were in a prayer meeting, after all—fear would just seem unholy!), but the tension in the room would always rise until we were certain that the building was not going to collapse.

We did what we could to help our neighbors with the rebuilding process, but it was slow going. The government, overwhelmed with requests for help, was unable provide much support, so people had to fix their houses themselves as best they could. The sight of neighbors pounding nails into their houses each day broke my heart, and I did what I could to help them, taking them meals and offering to watch their children when I could.

The trauma of the earthquake and Hamadan's limping efforts toward recovery overshadowed our final language examination in February. Dick and I were hard-pressed in the early weeks of 1958 to be able to study adequately. As the weeks wore on, the demands on our time grew exponentially, for in addition to our usual responsibilities and the new ones we took on as a result of the earthquake, we had to pack our things for our return to the Faraman orphanage. The McAnlises and the Heydenburks were preparing to start church-planting endeavors elsewhere in the country, and we, along with the Slaughters, were slated to take their places at the orphanage as soon as we had passed our final language exam.

Furniture on the Hillside

The final language examination was a blur, but we passeed with flying colors exactly two years to the week we had started language study. Then we had to finish packing, make a round of goodbye visits to our dear neighbors, and plan travel arrangements for our return to Faraman. Mr. Mirzai, our first language teacher, traveled to Hamadan by bus to help us move. Tubah and I boarded a bus to Faraman with the boys, leaving Dick, Mr. Mirzai, and our hired truck driver to navigate the dusty lack of roads to the orphanage.

We arrived the day before the truck, and Tubah and I spent the remainder of the day frantically cleaning out our new home. We needn't have hurried—the next day at dusk, we were startled by the sight of Mr. Mirzai strolling into the orphanage, hot and dusty, yet somehow retaining the unhurried demeanor characteristic of the culture.

"Where is the truck?" I asked him in Farsi, skipping customary pleasantries in my concern.

Mr. Mirzai took a swig of the water Tubah had run to bring him before turning to me. He seemed to be weighing his words carefully. "I need to take the orphanage trailer to pick up Dick and your things," he explained.

This seemed lacking as far as actual explanations were concerned. "Where *is* Dick?"

"With your luggage. The truck was climbing one of the large hills back there, and we hit a curve that was too sharp for the truck to pass." Mr. Mirzai took another sip of water as I tried to connect the puzzle pieces of his story into a coherent picture.

"So the truck is waiting on the hill?"

"No, no," Mr. Mirzai explained patiently. "The truck driver had to go back to Hamadan, so we unpacked the truck and put everything on the ground by the road."

My expression of horror must have translated well cross-culturally, for he rushed to explain, "Dick is with them. They are safe. We decided that Dick would spend the night guarding the things while I came here to get the trailer. I'll go back and pick him up as soon as I get it."

The trailer was in town until the next day, so a small group of Faraman farmers was dispatched to guard the stuff with Dick and I spend a fretful night praying that everyone would be ok. Those hills were primarily populated by thieves and mountain goats; while I felt Dick was equal to handling the latter, I remained concerned about the former.

It was noon the next day when the trailer finally pulled in, and Mr. Mirzai and I raced to greet it. It seemed to take an unusually long time to unload the goods purchased in town, and my hovering over the process was probably a hindrance, but I was determined to at least *feel* as though I was helping. It was a little after noon when Mr. Mirzai and a farmer finally took off in the trailer. Mr. Mirzai was the only man to return, with a full load of luggage.

"We'll have to take several loads," he explained in answer to my inquiring look. "There just wasn't enough room. I hope we'll finish today. But so far, no thieves," he grinned.

Tubah and I hurried to help him unload the trailer, then worked on unpacking what we could while Mr. Mirzai headed back for yet another load. It took four trips altogether, and I was relieved when I finally saw Dick come in with the final load.

"I was so worried!" I gave him a hug when he had finally entered the house, having made it through the crowd of villagers and orphans who had thronged to greet him. "How was it?"

"Oh, not too bad—just really cold." Dick stretched and yawned. "I tried not to sleep too much."

"I should hope so!" I arched an teasing eyebrow at him. "Are you sure nothing was taken?"

Dick shrugged with a grin and moseyed off to find a bed. I dug through our luggage to find some bedding to make up the mattress we had been sleeping on, but Dick was fast asleep long before I found it.

The new house was in many ways a pleasant departure from the one in Hamadan. There were five rooms, and, much to my delight, one of them was a bathroom—there would be no more unfortunately timed run-ins to our neighbor's house. Water was piped from a nearby hillside into the house, which was another wonderful addition (on our second day there, Tubah caught me excitedly turning the water in the kitchen on and off over and over, just to make sure it still worked). Dick once again plied his ingenuity and rigged up a few generator-powered electric lights in the kitchen and living room, and I deposited kerosene lamps throughout the rest of the house. The living room and bedrooms had been covered with a very thin layer of concrete, which was a step up from the mud floors in the kitchen and bathroom. The tin roof did not catch my attention until the Sunday morning when a rainstorm ripped it from the house. We recruited everyone who had come to church that morning to help us fix it, which they did by pulling the roof back into place and piling rocks on top of it. It remained that way for months before they did a real repair job on the roof, and I spent several weeks making mental wagers with myself regarding the odds of it staying in place.

Life in the Raw

There was no orientation into Faraman, nor would one have been possible. The events of each day varied, and seemed mostly comprised of circumstances for which no one would even think to prepare.

The orphanage was full to capacity when we arrived—there were 8 children in the baby room alone, and many of my mornings were spent there, helping the older girls in the orphanage change diapers and feed that never-satiated crowd. Then there were meals; Dick and I often did double-duty with regard to breakfast and lunch, supervising the orphans at each meal before heading back to our house to eat with Steve and Davy. Homeschooling Steve was beginning to take a turn for the better; Dick and I were careful to speak English to him whenever we were alone so that his ability to distinguish between the languages would improve.

Taking care of the children was one of the great joys of my life. The orphanage children nicknamed Dick and me within a few days of our arrival in Faraman, for they insisted that calling us "Mr. and Mrs. Corley" wouldn't work. "That's not how families do it!" I was dubbed 'Mommy Kuchek,' which translated to 'Little Mother.' (I was the successor to Alpha Heydenburk, who had been 'Big Mother'). Dick was 'Agha Jon,' which roughly translated as 'Dear Mister.' Motherhood had always been one of the primary desires of my heart, and while I had never imagined serving in that capacity for 46 children, I found that I quite enjoyed it. It was certainly full of unexpected moments; one bath day, for example, I was given the responsibility of bathing all the toddlers—by myself. We were short-handed, but the children hadn't been bathed yet that week, and Faraman was so dirty that waiting to bathe them simply was not an option. Five toddlers at once do not make for a smooth bathing experience, and I finally gave up and hopped in the tub with them, much to their glee.

We did our best to keep life at the orphanage from becoming too monotonous for the children; we had small group devotional times each night, dividing the children by age group and gender, and I cherished my opportunities to get closer to the older girls, whose lessons I taught. We showed evangelistic film strips during our Wednesday night Bible study time, which was often the highlight of the children's week. While we couldn't afford to take the children on big excursions, we would often walk down to the nearby river with them for a picnic, or spend evenings in compound-wide games of hide-and-seek or tag. On weekends we would sometimes load a whole group of them into our trailer and take them to play on the nearby mountains.

One of our favorite orphanage past-times was walking to the very top of a nearby hill, where the children's favorite hangout, dubbed "the tree," was located. That particular tree was a beloved symbol in Faraman--it was a bizarre sight, sitting alone at the top of a massive hilltop with no visible water source, and the villagers would often walk up the hill and attach written prayers to Allah to its broad branches. The presence of the tree provided us with tangible opportunities to talk about God's unseen presence (the villagers even called it 'the tree that God watered'), and to spark the children's curiosity regarding prayer.

Life with the kids was extremely busy and equally rich.

There were also down moments. The conditions would not have passed a cursory health inspection. The villagers' dogs spread fleas and lice with enviable generosity; I quickly tore up all my white socks to use as rags, for I couldn't handle looking down to find a flea colony collecting around my feet. We administered worm medicine frequently to all the children, yet still found ourselves in a constant battle against parasites. And each day, the iron entered my soul afresh against the thick dust and general filth that gave everything in the compound a drab appearance, despite my best efforts.

Two months after we arrived at Faraman, 23 of our 46 children came down with measles. It was one of the longest weeks of our lives; Joel, Sara, Dick, and I barely slept as we moved from one bed to another, delivering meals and comforting children. Shamsi, one of the babies, developed pneumonia, and had to be taken to Kermanshah hospital, three hours away; she recovered, but I insisted that she stay at our house upon her return so Tubah could keep a close eye on her.

The measles epidemic was barely passed when baby Davy became seriously ill, unable to keep down even the water I tried to spoon-feed him. We made yet another emergency trip to Kermanshah, and I spent 5 days struggling against tears as I watched Davy endure endless rounds of IVs. As soon as the unknown illness passed, I returned to Faraman to be met with the heart-breaking news that baby Shamsi had taken a turn for the worse and passed away during the previous night. It was gut-wrenching to bury a child. As much as I had tried to prepare for persecution on the mission field, I hadn't realized how emotionally taxing the "non-spiritual" ins and outs of daily missionary life could be.

"Doreen, I'm concerned about the babies," Sara told me a few weeks after Shamsi's death.

"More measles?" I looked quickly over at her.

"No, nothing like that."

"What then?"

"Have you noticed that they don't seem to be gaining weight?"

I cast my mind back. "Hm. . .now that you mention it, some of them are on the thin side."

"At first I thought it was just that they were still recovering, but it's been a few weeks, Doreen, and they're *really* thin still. I have no idea why that would be."

I didn't have answers for her, but we observed the babies carefully during the next few days, and she was definitely right. The babies looked extremely underfed, despite the fact that we would fill their bottles to bursting at each feeding. We could only conclude that something was wrong with the milk.

"Maybe Iranian cows make less nutritious milk," Sara suggested. "Because they eat less, or something."

When we went to Mr. Mirzai with our difficulty, though, he scoffed at our suggestion. "There's nothing wrong with Iranian cows; it's Iranian milkmen you have to watch out for. Do you boil your milk?"

"Of course." We were careful to pasteurize every drop of milk that came through the village. The last thing we needed was an orphanage full of food poisoning.

"And when you boil it, what happens?"

"What do you mean? It just. . .boils. Is that bad?" I felt my heart sink at the idea that I'd been unwittingly feeding the kids bad milk.

"If it were milk, it wouldn't just boil," Mr. Mirzai said quietly. "You have to watch real milk very carefully, because if it boils, it will boil over and get foam all over the stove and floor."

"Oh. So the milkman has been doing something to the milk?"

"Probably watering it down. Tomorrow I'll go into the village and watch how the milkman prepares the milk. He knows better than to steal from orphans." The gleam in Mr. Mirzai's eye made me grateful that I was not a dishonest milkman.

Mr. Mirzai returned the next day with news that the milkman had been watering the milk down dramatically; three-fourths water, one-fourth milk.

"He thought he could fool the foreigners," Mr. Mirzai said.

"He was right," Sara sighed, and I nodded, frustrated that we hadn't caught the culprit earlier.

"We can switch to another milkman if you want," Mr. Mirzai said. "But this one will never water the milk down again."

He didn't; every day after that, our milk boiled over, and in no time our babies were healthy, chubby versions of their former selves.

Clinic Duty

In addition to the duties with the children, we found that the Faraman compound had also developed a reputation for having a clinic. While this had been accurate enough in the era of medically-trained Harriet Burris, it became a gross exaggeration when Harriet moved on, leaving behind the medically-naïve Corleys and Slaughters. We managed to get a missionary nurse to visit the compound and teach us how to give shots to oranges, but once she left we found that giving shots to humans was a different matter entirely. Joel discovered this the hard way one day when he thrust a needle into a man's arm and yelped as he pushed the needle through the patient into his own thumb. Besides the penicillin shots we administered (more or less effectively), we felt qualified to give eye drops and worm medicine, and enthusiastically offered these three solutions to whatever malady might walk through the compound doors; some problems, however, were clearly beyond the expertise of our combined knowledge and the small medical book Harriet Burris had left for us.

One afternoon, a man from the village rushed in, flustered. Our language study had prepared us to speak a stilted, emotionless version of Farsi, and it took us a few minutes and the combined conversational powers of all four of us to understand what he was saying; his wife had given birth the night before, and the afterbirth had not yet been expelled.

Joel stared at Sara. Dick stared at me. Sara and I stared at each other, locked in a visual game of "rock-paper-scissors."

"I have no idea how to remove an afterbirth," I whispered to Sara.

"You've had more kids than I've had," she pointed out. Our reticence must have shown, for the poor man was becoming more and more frantic.

"I guess we'd better pray," Dick finally said, as Sara and I each remained rooted to the ground, unwilling to even attempt what would amount to blind surgery.

We all quickly agreed to this plan of action and gathered with the poor frazzled husband to lift the woman up in prayer. It was all we could do; I felt that the offer of eye drops wouldn't even have a placebo effect on the woman at this point.

We were relieved the man returned within the hour to report that the afterbirth had been expelled.

"I'm so glad!" I exclaimed when Sara ran in with the news. I'd spent that hour alternately praying and wondering if I should have attempted at least *something*, and guilt had started to set in.

"I'm only 27," I told Dick later that day. It seemed self-evident to me that untrained 27-year-olds shouldn't have to deal with grave medical problems.

Dick's eyes narrowed. "Yes. . .but we've been called here, Doreen. We need to do everything in our power to help everyone who comes across our path. In the name of Jesus."

I winced at his words. I did not always appreciate my husband's sugar-coating-free honesty. "I know, but—Dick. . ." I sat down at the kitchen table and held my head in my hands. "Don't you ever think this is crazy?"

He pulled a chair next to me, placing a gentle hand on mine. "Honey, has God ever let us down in the past?"

I shook my head. "No, Dick. But this is so hard sometimes! I feel like I'm in over my head right now. Nobody trained me to do any of this."

"I know, honey. God never said that following him would be easy. He just promised that he'd always be present to help us out."

Dick's matter-of-fact presentation was irritatingly truthful.

I sighed. "I know, love. I just get tired sometimes."

"Have you talked to God about it?"

I was brought up short. "Oh. . .well. . .I guess not, really."

That night I wrestled honestly with God. What was He expecting of me? Why would He put some of these responsibilities in my lap? Didn't He know I was unqualified? *Of course you're unqualified, Doreen. You forget to use my strength when you're confident about your work. But my power is made perfect in weakness.* It was a reminder I continued to need daily.

While medical problems were the scariest issues to deal with at the orphanage, they were not the most wearisome. That title was given unanimously to the arguments of the villagers whom we hired to work the land around the orphanage. We had good relationships with them, but they perpetually squabbled with each other. As the overseers of the Faraman orphanage, it fell to Dick and Joel to serve as mediators for the frequent arguments that cropped up between the farmers, usually with regard to boundary stones and the water supply. By the third such disagreement we realized that the culture's currency of disagreement was paid in revenge and grudges, and Dick and Joel became experts at developing compromises that left very few people happy, least of all themselves.

"But at least everyone is equally unhappy," I pointed out to Dick one night after a particularly intense discussion. He didn't find that sentiment as comforting as I'd hoped.

'Heavenly' Hospitality

Despite the occasional frustrations we encountered with regard to the villagers, we found ourselves largely overwhelmed by their hospitality. They had next to nothing, but were willing to sacrifice anything they did have for the sake of a guest. We were frequently invited to dine in the village; before each of these occasions, a member of the family with whom we would be dining would show up with the request that we send along plates and cutlery, as they did not have enough for everyone. I would pack up the requested number of items and send Tubah over to deliver them. At the appropriate time (a few hours after the stated time, of course) we would walk over to our friends' tiny house. The families always received us warmly, seating us on the carpets covering their dirt floors and providing us with as much food as they could afford, then stood in the background, quietly watching while we ate; it was their way of honoring us. In Iranian culture, conversation did not flow around mealtimes; food was intended to be enjoyed with as few distractions as possible. "Well, Mommy Kuchek," Tubah explained to me when I first asked about the dearth of mealtime conversations, "You can't think of Allah's gift of food if you talk to each other while you eat."

"Oh." *Well that would have been helpful before eating with Faraj.* I shook my head ruefully. Maybe one day this would all be second nature to me. Maybe.

It wasn't until we finished eating (carefully leaving enough so that the family could eat afterward) and the tea was brought around that the family would join us for long hours of conversation. They would wait until we left to eat dinner themselves. Their hospitality put everything I had seen up to that point to shame; their joy in self-sacrifice was astonishing. It became very clear within just a few weeks of arriving in Iran that Persians treated guests as people sent by God, and considered it their duty to honor the guest with whatever means and resources they had to offer. It was difficult for Dick and I to eat while we knew our friends were sitting, hungry, in the background, especially since we knew they did not have very much to give; but we knew it would hurt them deeply if we refused their hospitality, so we settled for expressing our deep appreciation for their service and returning the invitations as often as we could.

I told Dick after one such occasion, "Honey, I don't think I'll ever be able to come up with an excuse not to host people again." I had been known to say that "Our house isn't nice enough," or "We don't have enough food" when we had been struggling through school, but the villagers didn't have nice houses or large amounts of food, either, and yet they hosted often and joyfully. What's more, I was discovering that even if the trappings of such an evening were not perfect, it was possible to come home after a very simple meal in a hut saying, "What a great time we had!"

when the conversation had been stimulating and the company enjoyable.

We learned that the Iranian idea of small talk was much more free-form than the American idea. While Americans shied away from small talk of any great weight, Iranians relished intense political and religious discussions. One of the first times I went to an Iranian function, I had barely settled myself on the floor near the hostess when one of the other guests turned to me and asked, "Are you a Muslim yet?"

The question threw me off guard and I stuttered out an answer in my limited Farsi. A few more social interactions with Iranians convinced me that it was critical to develop some answer to that question, for it came up nearly every time I was visiting with an Iranian. It flowed into conversation as easily as a casual "How was your day?", and when I answered with a "No," they wanted to know why not. Finally, as I realized that Iranians connected with parabolic speech, I developed a sort of story to answer their questionings:

"If a man isn't hungry," I would explain, "he doesn't go out and look for a restaurant. I found something in Jesus that filled me up, so I am not looking for anything else, because Jesus made me full inside."

While this rarely settled the issue for them, it certainly piqued curiosity and led to many good conversations. I was very thankful that the Lord had given me such a helpful and intriguing answer to that oft-asked question.

The communication in that culture was very different than the more direct style of American speech. Conversation in Persia was an art form that Dick and I learned to appreciate. Unlike the sometimes brusque forms of address in the Midwestern United States, Iranians had a way of smoothly sidestepping a point until it was made.

For example, one day I realized that my watch had disappeared from its place on the bureau. I hurried to Tubah.

"Tubah," I said, "My watch is missing! I left it on the bureau, and I have no idea where it might be."

Tubah shrugged. "Zeinab may have taken it," she said, referring to our cleaning lady.

"I know. . .but Tubah, I'm not sure how to ask her about it. You know she won't forgive me if I sound like I'm accusing her."

"Here's what you do, Mommy Kuchek," she instructed. "Go to her and say, 'Zeinab, I'm so silly! I've taken off my watch, and I can't seem to find it anywhere! When you're cleaning today, if you find it, will you please just put it on the dining room table?' That way, she'll realize she was caught, but she'll be able to save face."

I was slightly skeptical, but sure enough, the watch magically appeared on the table within an hour of my conversation with Zeinab.

It was a difficult yet fascinating study to root out all the unspoken cultural nuances. In order to fit in, Dick and I had to educate ourselves on how to walk, how to drink tea, whom to greet in a room and in what order, where and how to sit upon entering a room, how to politely excuse ourselves at the end of an evening. .there was much to learn, far beyond simple language study. But with the help of our language helpers and very patient friends, Dick and I soaked up the cultural mores.

I realized one day, as I prepared food for a meal we were hosting that evening, that being a missionary had required far more of me than merely learning a language and preaching the gospel. In order to have any impact in Persian lives, we had to live incarnate in the Persian culture. We had to renounce all our claims on Americanism, we had to be willing to integrate Iranian culture into the very fiber of our beings if we were to have any integrity. In order to reach the Persians, we had to become Persian. *It's so much like Christ.* Just as He had renounced his rights as part of the Godhead to take on the identity of a human, we had to renounce our rights to comfortable American lives in order to take on identity as Iranians. It was a difficult, painful, beautiful process.

7 Babies and Blizzards

"Mommy Kuchek, I think I've gone into labor."

Our gatekeeper's wife, Taus, approached me after church one Sunday with the news. It was her first child, and since Sara and I were both pregnant at the time ("must be something in the water," we surmised), she had asked us to come along to help.

"Taus, I'll be right there," I promised, gesturing to Sara across the room.

I hurried home to ensure that my family was fed before I headed over to Taus' tiny one-room hut. The father and his friends were gathered at the doorway, waiting for news. I entered to find Taus surrounded by village women. To my surprise, she was standing up, her mother-in-law gently rubbing her back by the light of a kerosene lamp. The labor process was slow, and the room hot and close, but finally, Taus stooped over a large tray that had been covered with a towel and pushed the baby out, head-first, onto the tray.

"What is it?" I asked the lady next to me. She didn't answer. I asked again, and was once again ignored. Then it hit me. *It must be a girl.* My thought was confirmed when the father walked into the room, took one look at the faces gathered there, and then grimly walked back out. I understood the father's sentiment; in that culture, the boys were essentially their parents' social security. They could work and bring home wives to help their aging mothers. A family's entire future depended on having a boy. At the same time, however, my heart bled over the cold reception of that sweet little girl.

I received yet another piece of birth-related culture shock several weeks later, when the woman who baked bread for the orphanage knocked on our window at 4 AM one morning.

"What is it?" I asked her, flinging back the window.

"I just gave birth to my baby," she said. I knew that she had been pregnant with her fourth, and now that she mentioned it, she did look somewhat deflated.

"You just gave birth? Where is everyone?" I looked across the compound to her hut, expecting to see some sort of light or movement indicative of a gathering of people.

"I sent my husband and other children away for the evening," she explained. "It was my fourth, so it went quickly. I came to say that I don't think I'll be able to bake the bread today."

I stared at her, incredulous. *She just walked across the compound after giving birth to say she's going to be taking one day off?* "Oh, you can take more than one day," I hastened to assure her, but she shook her head. "Do you need help cleaning up?"

"No, I did that already."

I wrapped the conversation up as quickly as possible so she could hurry back to bed. I had spent up to a week in the hospital after each of my babies had been born; I couldn't imagine what it would be like to give birth alone, clean up, and then take a single day off before going back to work. These women were marvels.

Peril on a Mountain Pass

While these cultural forays were fascinating, I knew that I wasn't prepared to be *that* integrated into the culture, and we decided that it would be best for Sara and me to return to the well-equipped Hamadan hospital to give birth. Because of the miserable conditions inherent in traveling while extravagantly pregnant I decided to go a month early; my other two children had come early enough to warrant it. I decided to take Steve with me so that his schooling would not be interrupted, but David would have to stay behind, for I didn't want to burden our hosts, the Jaegers, unnecessarily. Sara was due shortly after me and agreed to watch over Dick and Davy until she came to join me in Hamadan.

Allen McAnlis and Clem Heydenburk, headed to Hamadan on a business trip, offered me a ride. While the tiny VW bug was not exactly a luxury vehicle, I did prefer it to having to deal with bus travel.

Stevie and I were accordingly packed into the back of the car on the first of March, 1959. Iran was still well within winter's grip, and before we had gotten very far, I heard the men conversing in suspiciously low tones.

"What's going on?" I asked them, trying to lean forward; my belly effectively prevented much movement on my part. I settled for projecting my voice when I repeated the question.

"There's snow on the mountain we have to cross," Clem told me. "We'll probably have to stop and put chains on the car."

Mountain travel was already somewhat nerve-wracking for me, especially after the debacle with our moving truck a few years before. *At least we know our car won't be too big*, I grinned to myself, though I didn't feel the need to share my thought aloud. Allen was touchy about his tiny car. We had only driven for another 15 minutes or so before the men decided that it would be safest to put chains on the car. They stepped into the cold and grunted and groaned while Stevie and I, ensconced comfortably inside, alternated between cheering them on and munching the sandwiches we had brought for lunch.

When the men had settled back into the car for their lunch break, however, I became suddenly aware that blackness was encroaching upon us. "Doesn't it seem a bit dark outside for lunchtime?" I asked. I rubbed at the car window with my sleeve, expecting that removing the accumulated steam would yield more light. I was wrong. Snow was swirling thickly around the car, obscuring most light and all vision.

The men put down their sandwiches and stared grimly out the window. "It's a white-out," said Allen.

"A blizzard?" Illinois had prepared me for cold weather, but I had never experienced anything this extreme.

"So it would seem." Clem rubbed his hand together and sighed. "We definitely can't drive in this," he said, lest that fact might have escaped the rest of us. "I know this road," he continued. "There's a tea house at the top, and we could wa-" he cut off the rest of his sentence as he spun in his seat and came face-to-belly with the most obvious complicating factor in our trip.

"How far is it?" I tried in vain to get a peek at the top of the mountain.

Clem shrugged. "I'm honestly not sure."

Climbing to the top of a mountain in the middle of a blizzard didn't exactly sound like a "can't-miss" opportunity to me, but after weighing the other options, we decided that it would be best for us to try. The promise of hot tea at the top of the mountain became more and more appealing as the car began a magical transformation into a refrigerator unit. Allen volunteered to stay with the car; if someone who was better equipped for snow travel passed by, he would try to get them to tow it up the hill. Otherwise, we might be stuck there for days.

With this arranged, Clem, Stevie and I bundled up and floundered out into the snow.

The car had been chilly. The great outdoors was downright frigid. My first sensation was the uncomfortable stickiness of my frozen mucous. My eyeballs were the second body part to protest, and they were quickly joined by my lungs, fingers, and toes. Clem took a firm grip on my arm and tramped off; I grabbed Steve in my turn, and we staggered up the slope with the assumed bravado of people with no other recourse.

It was bitterly cold; each breath I took was increasingly painful. I could feel the ice that had formed inside my coat clinking against my legs.

I looked up and caught a glimpse of lights in the distance. *The tea house! It must be close!* I rallied myself for a final push, but my urgency was preemptive. We turned a corner and the lights disappeared, taking my hope with them. I tried to speak encouraging words to Stevie, but I wasn't entirely sure my message was being conveyed; if the wind wasn't carrying away my words, my personal lack of confidence was probably puncturing the sense of support I was trying to convey.

I turned so that Stevie could hear me better, only to tumble into a snowdrift. *Lord, please let this be over now*, I prayed as Clem and Stevie frantically tried to help me up. I felt like a beached polar bear. By the time they hoisted me to my feet, I found myself fighting back tears. None of my platitudes were working, and I couldn't fight off images of becoming stuck interminably in a snowdrift.

Finally, we rounded a corner and to my relief I saw the tea house directly before us. We stumbled and slipped the last few steps to the door; Clem flung it open and ushered us in.

My hopes of finding comfort and safety dissipated. The room was tiny and windowless, and the tiny stove in the center filled the air with thick soot. The soot, in turn, was settling on and around the inhabitants of the tea house—all male, and all with less-than-welcoming expressions on their faces at the entrance of the astoundingly pregnant foreign woman and her son. I had the sudden recollection that women never visited Persian tea houses; my eagerness to get out of the cold had caused me a momentary memory lapse. Even though I knew that I could plead forgiveness based on extenuating circumstances, I still felt extremely uncomfortable as I timidly took in my surroundings.

Instead of chairs, the men in the tea house were sitting on a sort of ledge that was attached to the wall all the way around the room. It was several feet off the ground. I looked from my giant, rounded belly to the shelf, and could barely contain the hysterics that threatened to overwhelm me. If women were not welcome in tea houses, I could only imagine the effect a half-crazed pregnant woman might have on female-tea house relations for years to come. *Lord God*, I prayed in near-panic, *how in the world am I going to get on that shelf?*

Clem turned to me. "The man only has eggs and bread and tea." I had been too busy dealing with my private horrors to notice that Clem was bargaining with the proprietor. When he named the price of our meager meal, I could barely contain my gasp. Clem had been working in Iran for over 30 years and was an excellent barterer, but the tea house owner knew we were at his mercy, and the only price he would offer was absurdly high.

Stuck, Clem agreed to the terms of the agreement, and we were each given a straw mat to rest on while the tea house owner bustled about to prepare our eggs and tea.

Clem crawled up onto the shelf and reached down to help me. I managed to half-climb, half-roll my way up, and had barely settled myself when I was hit with yet another unfortunate realization. The owner had just approached with our meal, and I leaned down and asked him where the restroom was.

He eyed me doubtfully. "Well, there's a toilet across the street. . .but I don't think you should go there. You might get hit by a car or lost in the storm."

Good thinking! I don't think I should go there either! I barely kept my smart comments to myself. I could not afford to alienate the source of this important information.

The owner suddenly hit upon a solution. "Well, if you go out the teahouse door and walk around to the back, there's a place where you can go."

I thanked him and grabbed Stevie. "Honey, you're my ally," I told him as we slid off the shelf and headed back out into the bitter cold. Keeping my hand attached to the side of the tea house, I groped my way around to the back. We appeared to be entering some sort of cave.

All was dark inside, and as I took a moment to catch my breath, I was startled by a deep "Mmmm—ooooooooo" that emanated from my right. This set off a chorus of bleating. I sniffed the air. We were definitely in a stable.

I felt a giggle brewing in my belly, but I clamped a lid on it. While the absurdity of our situation certainly called for a good laugh, any hint of mirth now would lead to a frenzy of emotional catharsis, and that was a luxury I could not afford quite yet. *You can laugh and cry about this as much as you'd like later*, I promised myself. As Stevie and I made our unsteady way back to the tea house, I was struck by the parallels between my situation and the nativity story.

As I thought about the cramped, dark, and smelly stable we had just exited, I cringed a little. Giving birth in such an environment was almost unthinkable, and I felt a new sort of gratitude for the Incarnation. I maneuvered my massive belly over a snowdrift, filled with the dread that my story might parallel Mary's to an even greater extent. *Lord, please let us get out of here. I don't want to have my baby here. . .and yet. . .Father, I guess if your child could be born in a stable, mine could, too*, I prayed. Having settled things as far as I was able, I stumbled back into the tea room to struggle back to my place on the shelf.

Allen had arrived while I was gone, having found someone to tow the tiny car up the hill. He and Clem helped me onto the ledge before Clem fell asleep. Allen managed to stay awake, and his help was invaluable, as I was continually needing to hop off the ledge and head to the stable, poor Stevie in tow. After one of these expeditions I settled myself against the wall, squirming every few minutes as the position became increasingly unbearable. Allen leaned over to me.

"Doreen, if we weren't here, I would give you a backrub, but I don't dare."

I knew that Allen, a missionary doctor's son, had probably seen situations like this often. Though his empathy didn't quite make up for the missing backrub, I appreciated it nonetheless.

The night dragged on miserably. In between my far-too-frequent trips to the stable and subsequent efforts to heave myself back onto the ledge, I drifted in and out of restless sleep, desperately wishing that the night would be over, the storm would stop, and we would eventually arrive in Hamadan; hope was at a low ebb.

Stranded travelers continued to arrive in the tea house throughout the night. Each time I heard the door open I cocked open one sleepy eye to assess the new displaced traveler. I jerked to full attention, however, when a truck driver entered with his collapsible cot. Allen and I watched in silence as he set it up, then stretched out with a long sigh to sleep.

Allen leaned over to me with a smirk. "Doreen, thou shalt not covet thy neighbor's bed."

"Allen," I told him mournfully, "it's too late."

Finally, as dawn began to creep over the land, the roar of the storm dulled, then stopped altogether. Armed with that peace of mind (as well as dehydration and exhaustion) I was finally able to fall asleep.

"Doreen," Clem whispered, gently shaking me awake. "The roads are clear. We can go."

I jerked awake and rubbed sight into my bleary eyes. "We can?" I was almost afraid to hope. I yearned for the cramped but comparatively comfortable backseat of the VW. *That'll teach you to be ungrateful,* I told myself ruefully, remembering my attitude regarding the cramped car at the beginning of the trip. Clem helped me off the ledge one final time and we headed out into the cold morning.

We crossed the road to where Allen was warming up the car. "Doreen, look!" He pointed into the ravine that ran along the street. I peeped in—there lay the toilet the proprietor had warned me against using. Apparently a truck, unable to stop in the snow, had hit it during the night. For approximately the seventh time that trip, I bit back the emotions that threatened to escape in hysterical laughter. The stable experienced a sudden increase in its relative value as a bathroom.

We piled into the car yet again, and I mercifully fell asleep, waking only as we finally pulled up to the Jaegers' house in Hamadan. Belle Jaeger flung open the courtyard door in answer to my knock.

"Hello, hel--" Her jaw dropped mid-sentence when she caught sight of my face. In a move that I felt was not entirely diplomatic, she threw back her head and began to laugh.

"Belle," I told her sternly, "I have been traveling for 29 hours. What are you laughing at?"

Belle, unable to fit a decipherable answer around her giggles, beckoned me inside, where she guided me to a mirror. Black smears had taken up residence in my eyes, nose, and the corners of my mouth. I looked as though I had spritzed myself lightly with soot before embarking upon my travels. Even I had to grin, albeit reluctantly, at the sight. My fellow travelers and I had not even noticed our relative state of grime, since we were equal partners in filth.

We had made it, however, and after a long bath and nap, I was ready to settle into life at Hamadan. It passed pleasantly enough, though I was a bit put-out by the fact that after all our efforts to make it to Hamadan in time for an early delivery, my third baby was the first one to arrive exactly on the due date; on March 27, 1959, Timothy Paul was born.

Dick was planning to travel to Hamadan at the end of March, so we decided not to bother sending him news of the birth. Four full days after Tim's birth, therefore, Dick arrived at the Jaegers to discover that he had a new son. He could not stay long, as he had to hurry back to the orphanage to keep it running. He took Stevie with him to make my trip back easier, but brought Sara along as an exchange, and I was happy to have someone to spend my days with until I had healed enough to return to my beloved life in Faraman.

Return Home

Life in Hamadan was not immune to the same sorts of bizarre problems that beset us in Faraman. Just two days after Dick left to return to the orphanage, Sara and I were spending a quiet afternoon in the apartment we'd borrowed from two teammates in Hamadan.

"Doreen, what's on the walls!?" Sara yelped.

I was startled out of rocking Tim gently to sleep. "What's the matter?" A quick glance rendered my question irrelevant. Water was pouring down the walls. I became suddenly aware of the sounds of a rainstorm outside. "Oh no! The apartment is flooding!" I lay Tim down and heaved myself to my feet, cursing Hamadan's flat roofs.

"We have to save the furniture!" Sara cried in the emotional frenzy of the extremely pregnant. I stared at her. I wasn't sure what sort of fight a one-hundred-pound woman who had just given birth and a bulgingly pregnant woman could wage against the heavy furniture that was dotting the room.

Sara waddled to a chest of drawers and placed her shoulder against it. "Come on, Doreen!"

"Well, Sara, maybe this will make your baby come quicker." I gave in and hurried to help her. We spent the next hour or so maneuvering heavy furniture away from the walls, then scurrying around to find every possible container to catch the water leaking through the roof. Sara wheezed and waddled. I prayed not to hemorrhage. Tim slept. Sara's baby didn't come, but the furniture was saved.

Two days later Tim and I took our return trip to Faraman, which stood in stark contrast to the agony of my trip to Hamadan. I was thrilled to look out the plane window and see my welcoming committee—Dick, Tubah, and Davy. It had been almost six weeks since I had seen my middle son, and when I rushed off the plane and tried to gather him into my arms, he pulled away.

"Come here, David," I coaxed, but the two-year-old clung to Tubah and eyed Tim with skepticism. I had to hand Tim off to Dick before David would even consider coming to me, and it took another few days before he either forgave or forgot my long absence and subsequent reappearance with a supplanter.

All in all, I was happy to find that life in the orphanage agreed with me.

"Dick, I'm so glad God brought us to the country," I told him one night in one of our rare moments of down time. "I don't really like living in big cities."

Dick wiggled his eyebrows at me. "That's where the people are, honey."

I shrugged. Dick's logic was irrefutable, but--*Lord, I would rather stay out of large cities from now on*, I told Him. He didn't listen at all.

8 Kohinoor: "Mountain of Light"

Just a few months later, we were called into a meeting by the field leaders of our mission. Rumors had been swirling regarding some big changes that were going to take place at the orphanage, but I had been too busy to pay much attention.

Given the general transience and instability of missionary life, however, I was only mildly surprised to find that the rumors were true: the older kids had outgrown the tutor we hired to teach at Faraman, so it had been decided that they needed to move to the nearby city of Kermanshah to attend public school. The Corleys had been elected as the number one choice to take them.

My mouth dropped open as the field leaders explained the proposed plan to us. The Burrises and Jaegers would move to Faraman to stay with the younger children while Dick and I would took the 25 school-aged children into Kermanshah for the school year. I could hardly imagine what it would be like to run such an operation on our own. Though we tried to stick to a general time schedule at the orphanage, we definitely had the freedom for flexibility, if needed—truth be told, anything but absolute flexibility was a luxury. If we moved to Kermanshah, that would mean getting at least 25 children up, fed, dressed, and out the door to school by 8:00 every morning, in addition to caring for our own three. God's sense of humor astounded me. *God, You know that I always wanted to be a mother*, I thought. *But this is a bit much!*

"Well, Dick, I opened wide my mouth, and He certainly filled it," I told my husband sardonically later that evening. "When I prayed that I could be a mother, maybe I should have suggested a specific number."

Dick laughed. "Yeah, that may not have been a bad idea. . .but I think this will be a good change," he added. While Dick had been a bedrock of the orphanage since we got there, I knew that his heart was to reach the Iranian people for Christ and I knew that significant element of his passions had not yet been tapped; moving to a bigger city could be a step in that direction.

In June of 1959, Dick and I headed to Kermanshah to find a house for ourselves and the children, who would join us in September.

Once the plans were in place, I became enthusiastic about the move. I enjoyed starting new projects, and Dick excelled at it. We had our first furlough back to the States coming up following that school year, and I knew I would enjoy trouble-shooting the first attempt at this new set-up before we returned to our beloved homeland for 14 months.

'Little Mother' to Many

We were blessed to find the perfect house shortly before our moving date in June. It was a beautiful building, with a balcony running the length of the second story, large decorative pillars, and a central stone-paved courtyard with a swimming pool. One of the best parts of it, though, was the location—one wall ran exactly along the courtyard of the American hospital in Kermanshah, while another was next to the Presbyterian compound where the local church building stood. The front wall faced *Pahlavi Avenue*, a major thoroughfare in the city named after the Shah. I was particularly thrilled by the proximity to the hospital. As the "mother" of 25 orphans and three little Corleys, I suspected that we would be its favorite "customers." We dubbed the house Kohinoor, or "Mountain of Light."

The house did need a lot of work, and we spent our summer ordering bunk beds for the children, cleaning the house and yard, and hiring a cook and laundry lady to help us with our brood. Dick began preaching at the local church, while I enjoyed the opportunity to start a ladies' Bible study for some of the local women. Dick and I also put together a curriculum for and hosted a youth conference in our big home before the children from the orphanage arrived. There were about 11 youth who were able to come each day and stay for the majority of the teaching, and we were thrilled to find our night services filling up to more than 100 people!

Despite the heavy load of the summer, we managed to squeeze a vacation out of the little time we had between the youth conference and the arrival of the Faraman children to Kohinoor. We invited the McAnlises to join us on a trip to our favorite Iranian vacation haunt—the Caspian Sea.

It was our third or fourth trip to that particular sea since we had moved to Hamadan, and we enjoyed them more each time we went. That area of Iran was particularly beautiful, and after the hustle and bustle of the orphanage, we relished the opportunities to get away and spend time playing as a family. This time, Allen McAnlis used his connections as a teacher in an Iranian school to gain access to an unused schoolhouse located on the very shores of the sea. Between our relatively nice accommodations and the fact that the McAnlises brought their cook along with them, freeing us from the burden of meal preparations, we felt very spoiled indeed, and returned to Kermanshah rested and as prepared as possible to become parents to 25 new children overnight.

"Is She your Mother?"

The children moved in and plunged the house into chaos.

The Iranian education system was much stricter than I had anticipated—the children came home after a long day of school only to spend the majority of their evenings working their way through the piles of homework that inundated them. The age range proved a struggle, to say the least—to have 25 children of both genders ranging in ages from 7 to 17 under one roof was complicated at the best of times.

I ran into an unanticipated concern when I realized that our sons might not grasp that Dick and I were their *actual* parents. While Dick led Corley family devotions every morning and we set aside a part of our afternoon to have tea and cookies with our boys, I still suspected at times that the Corley boys had no idea that we were their biological parents.

I also wanted our orphans to be able to know God's love and acceptance of them through the way Dick and I treated them. I took every opportunity I could to communicate to them that they were part of a family.

One day a little boy named Aziz came home from school in tears, a huge gash decorating his face.

"Aziz, honey, what happened?" I asked him, quickly creating a makeshift bandage for him out of some of the white sheeting we tried to always have on hand.

A big tear welled up in his eye, spilling over as he began to talk. "I was r-r-r-running around the corner of the building to get away from Hooman, and when I ran around the corner, I knocked heads with another little b-b-b-boy." The tears were coming faster now.

I thanked the man who had been so kind as to walk Aziz home, then hurried with the boy around the corner to the hospital. "You may have to get stitches," I told him as we walked. "I know that you will be very brave."

Aziz nodded. We entered the waiting room and took a seat across from two middle-aged men. They stared at us, but I was so accustomed to attention that I ignored them. It became more difficult when they began whispering between themselves and pointing at us, but I persisted in being stubbornly blind to their attention.

Suddenly one leaned over. "Excuse me," he said, "are you that boy's mother?"

I glanced down at Aziz, sniffling by my side, then looked the man directly in the eye. "Yes, I am," I said firmly.

The man looked a bit taken aback. "But how can you be? He doesn't look at all like you!"

Then why ask? I swallowed my tart response and paused in search of another.

"Well, sir, what does a mother do?" I finally responded. "A mother takes care of her children, makes sure they are fed and have clean clothes, takes them to the doctor when they need it, and disciplines them when they need it. A good mother loves her children. I do all that for Aziz. I am Aziz's mother." I gave the boy a comforting squeeze on the shoulder as I spoke, hoping that my words were having an impact on his lonely, orphaned heart.

The men, still slightly confused but chastened, finally settled back in their seats.

I also tried to make sure each child felt special; it was difficult to spend quality one-on-one time with each one, but I did my best. During periods of time when it was impossible to check in with each one separately, I would try to do something for groups of them. If we had cake one night for dinner, and there was extra left over, I might take a stack of plates and forks to the girls' room at bedtime, telling them not to tell the boys that they had gotten a special treat. Another night, the boys might get a similar delicacy. We made a big deal about each child's birthday, so that they each had at least one day when they stood out from their 'siblings'. (The children who didn't know what day was their actual birth date were allowed the luxury of choice, though we had to put some limits on it when some of them tried to sneak in two or three birthdays throughout the year). While there were little squabbles and such among the children, they so desperately wanted to belong that they created their own family within the compound.

My heart swelled with joy the day I heard a neighbor child say scornfully to one of our orphans, "How can *you* be an orphan? You have a family!"

Thank you, Lord, that these children are not growing up feeling neglected and lost, by you or by others!!!!!!

The conditions of our new house weren't much better than at Faraman; the night before Easter, we hid Easter eggs all over our house and the Presbyterian compound next door. We hadn't counted on the mice, though, and a substantial number of the eggs had been eaten by morning. Doris Bond, the nurse who came to help us out, became a fast friend and ally in our continuous battles against everything from intestinal worms to disobedience to head lice.

As we settled into the house and our new routine, I found that I liked life at Kohinoor; I was even able to overlook the fact that it was in a city.

Doreen Corley

A Change of Plans

"Folks, I have an announcement to make." Allen McAnlis had to raise his voice to be heard over the chatter as we settled in to the prayer meeting.

"When we come back from the States, I'll be sure to bring you some caramel candy," I was telling Sara. I was so excited about our upcoming furlough that I had probably promised to bring back entire suitcases full of stuff for other people, but I didn't care. I was going *home*!

Allen cleared his throat and waited as I grabbed a *shirini nargili* and turned to listen. "Sorry Allen." I smiled mischievously at him as I took a bite of my coconut macaroon.

Allen paused, staring at the floor for a moment, then heaved a sigh. The room stilled as a premonition of *something* swept in. I glanced at Sara and mouthed "What's going on?" She shrugged. Our little community was so tightly knit that I'd never experienced a surprise announcement. Rumors always preceded even the slightest change.

"Folks, as you know, Harriett and I have been serving as field leaders for decades now. We've really enjoyed our time with you, but. . ." Allen choked up. The "but" expanded to fill the air around us, depriving the room of oxygen. "I'm afraid that as of June, Harriett and I will be resigning from the mission."

A whooshing noise drowned the silence as everyone let out their breath in disbelief.

"What?"

"Why?"

"You can't go!"

I sat silently in the general hubbub, trying to grasp what Allen was saying. He and Harriett were. . .staples in our mission. I couldn't imagine the field without them. . .I suddenly bolted upright as the full weight of

Allen's decision struck me.

I stole a look at Dick. His lips were tight, but he met Allen's gaze steadily.

But, Allen, what about our furlough?! I was scared to ask. We were less than a year away from our first furlough—we had already lived in Iran for nearly four years. During that time, my younger sister had eloped, among other changes, and I desperately wanted to be able to go home and provide a season of support for my dear mother. But our furlough was contingent on one thing—the McAnlises had been slated to take over our position at Kohinoor during our year of furlough. If they stepped down, there was nobody else who would be able to take over. Furlough wasn't optional as far as we were concerned. We needed to go back and talk to supporters to raise our support for another term. We had even planned to take Mr. Mirzai back with us, as well, in hopes that he too could raise support for his desperately needed evangelism work.

"Honey, what are we going to do?" Dick asked me that night. He walked up behind me and began rubbing my shoulders, staring thoughtfully ahead.

"I don't know, Dick," I said, but the knot in my throat contradicted my words. There was a solution. It just happened to be one that I hated. *Say it,* my brain commanded my mouth. I tried to swallow back my emotion, but the tears came anyway. "Dick. . .you could go with Mr. Mirzai." I looked down at the floor, thankful that Dick was behind me so he couldn't see my face. "We have to go back and talk to our supporters, and we have no idea when the next opportunity will come."

Unfortunately, it was true. We had to take this furlough, and sending Dick and Mr. Mirzai alone while I held down the fort at Kohinoor appeared to be the only option.

Though I had proposed the plan, and even though my head told me that this was the most logical way, my heart was in protest. I didn't want to be left behind. I didn't want to have to care for all the orphans alone. I didn't want the boys to have to be without their father for months, and I certainly didn't want to be without my husband for that span of time! Most of all, I ached to see my family again. I was driven regularly to my knees. *Lord, why is this happening?* I asked him. I wanted answers, and I hated having to wait for them.

Even as I went about my daily routines, mothering my children, running the orphanage, and helping Dick prepare for furlough, my heart cried out against the situation. It wasn't so much the difficulty of the problem as the ease of the solution that bothered me. I simply could not understand why God would allow this to happen, when He had all the resources necessary at His disposal to pave the way for me to be able to visit home. I knew that God could easily change Allen's heart. I knew that He could supernaturally intervene to bring a couple into the picture who would be perfect to take on our roles for a year. And I knew that God was good. My difficulty was in reconciling a good and loving God with a God who was apparently refusing my request for something that felt so easy on His end and so important on mine.

I wrestled with God, while He, in His goodness, kept reminding me of His character.

God, I don't understand how You could do this.

Doreen, read Psalm 136; what does it say about My love for you?

God, I'm so angry right now.

Doreen, read Psalm 121. Where does your help come from?

God, I just want to go home!!!!

I know, Doreen. I do.

And God, I'm scared.

Doreen, look at your life! I've never left you yet, have I? What makes you think I will now? I'm not going anywhere, but I really want you to trust that.

There were days when the only thing that could bring peace and rest to the tumult of my mind was the act of praying through the Psalms, and I returned to them often, as much as to lament my situation before the Lord as to receive His answers.

Then, two weeks before Dick and Mr. Mirzai were to leave, Allen McAnlis once again stood up during a field meeting. "Many of you know that Harriett and I have been considering resigning from our position here in Iran, for a number of reasons," he began. I felt a tightening in my chest that I fought against.

Lord, forgive me for my frustration. I'm trying to trust You. I know You'll take care of me.

"Well, in the past few weeks, a few things have come to our attention to make us reconsider. . .'"

Oblivious to the rest of Allen's speech, I turned to Dick, trying to keep my hope from showing. Maybe, just maybe, there was time enough for us to reset our plans. Dick winked at me, and the bubble of hope growing inside me burst, sending rays of excitement through my body. *I might get to go home!!!!*

Allen had stopped talking and sat down, and Dick leaned into the lull that followed as everyone was trying to assimilate the new information: "Does that mean that all the Corleys can go on furlough?"

The answer was a resounding yes, and I left the meeting feeling lighter than I had in months. The moment we got back to Kohinoor, I hurried to our bedroom to have a conversation with God.

Thank You, Lord! Thank You, thank You, thank You!!!!! I know that I don't deserve this. I know I've been ungrateful and pouty the last few months. I know that You can and would have taken care of me and the boys while Dick was away. But what a blessing You've just given me!!!

It would be months, even years, before I would be able to comprehend the depth of the lesson God had been teaching me through those hard months of uncertainty: He would take care of me; no matter how my life circumstances did or did not align with what I had hoped for, He would always be there, and what He chose would be the best available option.

All I could think about at that point was that, after five long years away and a few months of deep uncertainty, I was finally going home!

9 "I Thought We Were Coming Back to America!"

"Doreen, are you ready?" Dick stepped into the room where I was frantically putting the finishing touches on one final bag.

"I am. Here it is!" I handed the bag over the Dick. "That one is for Badry, so keep it separate," I advised.

Dick nodded and headed to place the bag of the two-year-old who was being adopted by a Pennsylvania family in the car with the rest of our stuff.

I took one final glance around the room. The kids were out in the car already, and not having them underfoot was making my final sweep of the place a lot easier. "I still can't believe I'm traveling to the States with three children under the age of three," I grinned wryly to myself as I shut off the light and stepped outside. I had a feeling that the next 48 or so hours of my life were going to feel exponentially longer.

Compounding my fear was the fact that we were flying out of Tehran via *Syrian-Arab Airlines*. Jets hadn't been crossing the Atlantic when we first went to Iran, so this development had exciting (if terrifying) implications for our future furloughs. Having barely made my peace with other modes of transportation in Tehran, I was more than a little concerned about this turn of events. During our first taxi ride through that city, I found myself covering my eyes in horror as we jerked through the narrow, crowded streets at breakneck speed. When Omer Burris had asked me what was wrong, I told him pertly that "I don't want to see what kills me." I could only imagine what kinds of terror a Tehran-trained pilot might be able to evoke in me.

We got through the first two legs of the journey (driving to Tehran and flying to London) with relative ease, and I made the mistake of taking a sigh of relief when we reached our gate at the Heathrow airport. *Good, the hard part is over!* I should have recalled from the last 5 years of my recent history that hard parts tend to occur when you least expect them, but alas, I had forgotten that minor detail.

We loaded into the plane without incident (well, with as few incidents as traveling with four children, three of whom were under the age of three, will allow) but I noticed after I settled into my seat that the weather was far from ideal.

Dick had noticed, too. "Does it seem stormy out there? Do you think we should be flying in this?"

I leaned over to peek out the window at the rain sleeting across the tarmac. "It does seem pretty bad. But isn't London always rainy? Maybe these British pilots are really comfortable flying in storms."

I didn't realize that I had just uttered the understatement of the decade—as the plane rolled down the runway and finally lifted into the air, we felt a sudden jolt, followed by an ear-shattering pop. The lights flickered. I gripped my seat with both hands. Beside me, Badry let out a wail. I glanced out the window and muffled my own cry of fear. Flames were shooting out of the wing*!*

The entire plane was in uproar. The people who weren't moaning or praying had frozen into white-knuckled wax replicas of their former selves.

The intercom crackled and a soothing, British-accented voice came on. "Ladies and gentlemen, we appear to have been struck by lightning."

Horror washed over the cabin's occupants in a collective gasp.

"But the fire has gone out on its own, and as far as we can tell, there's no damage," the pilot continued. "So we're going to continue to our final destination. Hopefully there will be no further incidents, and we wish you a pleasant flight." His voice hadn't wavered once throughout the announcement, and I half-expected him to end it with a blithe "Cheerio!"

I really wondered how the pilot had assessed for damage from the cockpit, but it didn't seem my place to ask. As it turned out, though, he was correct, or at least correct enough to get us to New York. The rest of our flight occurred without incident—if, of course, one overlooked the fact that the entirety of the cabin's occupants was waiting with bated breath for a wing to fall off or a duck to get caught in the engine or any number of other problems that seemed as improbable as getting struck by lightning.

We couldn't get off the plane fast enough, but our rush was precipitous—no one from the mission was there to meet us. "I have a phone number for the mission," Dick assured me. "I'll go call them."

I nodded gratefully and sank down on a nearby chair, cradling Badry, trying to corral Davy, and directing Steve to hold Tim. *Help is on the way*, I reminded myself over and over as Badry refused to be comforted, Tim wriggled frantically to get out of my arms, and Davy kept Steve busy chasing him around the baggage claim.

Dick returned from his phone call, frustration written into the lines on his face. "Doreen, I can't work the telephone."

"What do you mean?" I couldn't fathom what he was trying to tell me. It was a telephone. Surely the man who could rig up a running water system for an entire village could work a telephone.

"I can't figure it out. I picked up the phone, and there was no dial tone, no operator, no nothing. It must be broken."

I heaved myself to my feet. "Let me see if I can figure it out." I knew that if Dick hadn't been able to, the chances of me miraculously decoding the key to the technology were slim, but I was willing to give it a shot. We moved all the children and our baggage to the nearby phone booth. I picked up the phone and tentatively asked for the *markaz*, but America's operators were either nonexistent or noncompliant. Dick and I traded hypotheses regarding how to use the device, but nothing seemed to work.

"I think we'll just have to ask somebody," I concluded, flagging down a passerby. "Excuse me, sir, can you explain to us how to use the telephone?"

I could only imagine what was going through the man's mind as he surveyed the ragtag "not quite foreign, but decidedly different" family before him, but he graciously followed me to the phone booth.

"Do you have a quarter?"

"Um. . .no." As his expression wavered toward judgment, I rushed to explain. "Well, you see, sir, we just got back from 5 years in Iran, so we haven't had a chance to change our money over to American bills yet." His expression lightened a bit, and I decided not to inform him that I didn't know that the telephone cost money; I had completely forgotten the American system. In Iran, it was never a problem to run into a shop and ask to use their telephone.

"Here, I think I have one." The man produced the desired coin and slipped it into the coin slot while Dick I watched intently. "Now, what number do you need?" Dick showed him the number, and the man dialed through, explaining the procedure as he went.

"Now you wait for them to pick up, and talk into it like this." He demonstrated the exact use of a telephone receiver while I flushed crimson. *We must look really, really, behind the times if he thinks we've never even spoken into a telephone! What does he know about Iran, anyway?* I was humbled by the recollection of my first response to Dick's suggestion that we go to Iran— *Iran? Where's that?.*

The man handed the receiver over to Dick and set off on his way, trailed by a chorus of profuse thanks.

The mission sent someone to pick us up, and within a few short hours we were comfortably tucked into bed in the mission office guest rooms, thankful that the most arduous leg of our trip was accomplished.

"Mom?" I jerked awake to find myself face-to-face with David, who was shaking my shoulder. "What is it, honey?" I sat up and tried to squint at the clock on the wall, but it was too dark to see anything.

"Mommy, is it morning?"

"I. . .uh. . .don't know, honey. Let's go into the kitchen so we don't wake up daddy."

"I'm awake, Doreen."

I glanced next to me. Dick was staring wide-eyed at the ceiling. "I've been up for at least 30 minutes."

"Oh. Well--" I reached over to flip on the light and check the time. "It's 3 o'clock!" I peeked out the window to double-check. It was definitely still morning. "Should we try to go back to sle--"

Davy set up a wail immediately seconded by Badry.

"Gang's all here!" Dick announced with a grin.

"Mommy, I'm *hungry*."

Dick and I shared a nod and shrug. We were both pretty hungry—come to think of it, we hadn't had anything to eat since we'd arrived in America.

"I guess we should just do an early breakfast. Or late dinner. What is a meal eaten at this time of day called?"

The kids voted unanimously that we call it breakfast, and I hurried to scramble some of the eggs we found in the mission office fridge, while Dick set about making toast. I had never seen a meal end so quickly—by the time Dick and I sat down to eat, Steve and Davy were already blinking violently over their half-eaten food and Tim had given up altogether and fallen asleep in his eggs.

Given the circumstances we decided to shut off our alarm clock and sleep in, and all of us were dead to the world until well past 1 o'clock that afternoon. Our odd sleep rhythms continued for several days, baffling us.

"Oh, that's normal," someone at the mission office assured us when we finally confessed our difficulty sleeping. "It's called jet lag. Since you crossed all those time zones so quickly, your bodies need time to catch up."

Dick and I had never heard of this phenomenon. Traveling to Iran by boat had afforded us plenty of time to acclimate to the new time zone by the time we'd arrived. I had the feeling this wasn't going to be the last thing about furlough that caught me by surprise.

I was right. We set off a few days later, stopping briefly in Pennsylvania to settle Badry in with her new family, who happened to be some supporters of ours. We then continued to my mom's house in Illinois. I could not wait to see her again—ever since Dad had died, I craved the chance to be a support and help to her, and I couldn't wait to be able to offer that support in person.

We pulled up in front of the tiny house where I had grown up, and I launched myself out of the car almost before it stopped, running in to give my mom a bear hug. Jackie, Pat, and their husbands and children formed a surprise welcoming committee, and we all chattered eagerly as we gathered together that evening.

Stevie and his cousins became inseparable after an initial period of shyness, and while Davy and Tim were a bit overwhelmed and over-stimulated by the newness of everything, they seemed interested, if not actively engaged, in all the activity.

As soon as we arrived Stevie asked for a drink of water, and my mom led him to the kitchen to get him a glass. A second later, I heard her cry out for me, and I hurried after them.

Stevie was standing above a puddle of water, an empty glass in his hands, consternation on his face. My mom was standing in front of him, equally befuddled.

"Doreen, what happened here?" She pointed to the water on the floor.

"Mama, I was done with the water, so I threw the rest on the floor," Stevie said by way of explanation. I looked from the soaked linoleum to my mother's startled face and burst out laughing.

"Well, honey," I told Steve, "in Iran I tell you to throw your water on the floor because it's brick and that way we can get the dust to settle. But here, the floors are made of something else, so if you don't want your water here anymore, you can throw it in the sink." *Oh boy, this is going to be a long furlough.*

Our life quickly settled into a routine. While I had expected to encounter culture shock upon my arrival to Iran, I had not been prepared for the reverse shock of re-entering America. I thought I'd return to the America of my memories, but the country had changed quite a bit in the five years that we had been gone, and adjusting to those changes took some mental gymnastics and a great sense of humor.

While doing the dishes one day, for example, I grabbed the bottle of blue dish soap and read the instructions: "One cupful per pan." *A whole cup for one pan of dishes?!* I was appalled. *We would never use that much in Iran.* Feeling very frugal and a little self-satisfied, I carefully measured out a half-cup full, reasoning that I could always put more soap in if necessary. I flipped on the water and turned around to gather some of the dishes from the table. In the 12 seconds it took me to get to the table, pick up some dishes, and turn back around, the suds were brimming out of the sink, trailing down the cabinets, and piling soft bubbles onto the floor. Dropping the dishes back on the table, I scrambled to turn off the tap and find a towel with which to mop up the suds. *Why didn't it work?* I picked up the bottle to double check the directions. *One CAPful per pan?!* In hindsight, that made much more sense. I made a quick vow to remember to read English directions as carefully as I read Farsi.

Just a few days later, I headed a few blocks away to the Laundromat where my mother did her laundry. I couldn't wait to use an automatic machine after all the time I'd spent hand-cranking each item through the tiny machine we had in Iran. I flung open the Laundromat door and stepped in, struggling to balance our huge load of laundry. Approaching one of the machines, I set my basket down and felt a jolt. *Wait. . .is this. . .the washer, or the dryer?* I bent over and studied the machine closely, but I couldn't quite tell. I snuck a glance at the woman to my right. She was pulling wet clothes from one of her machines. *Oh, good. Washer. That was easy.*

Feeling an unwarranted degree of pride at my sneaky problem-solving, I opened the door of the washer and stopped again, my smugness dissolving. I still had no idea how to use the machine in front of me.

Chagrined, I looked around the laundromat at all the other people, many of whom were dressed in the same style as I. *I probably look so normal to these people,* I realized. *But I'm about to ruin* that *illusion. I have no idea how to do this.* I spent the next several moments standing over my washer, pretending that I was sorting clothes while really trying to decipher the unhelpful instructions printed on the machine and surreptitiously watching other patrons load their laundry. *Oh, that lady did separate loads. Hm. . .that one put the soap in first, then the coin. What button did she push?* I felt terribly out of touch. *I need to find some way to brand 'I've been in Iran for five years!' to my forehead,* I decided. *Or perhaps I just need to start asking for help using a thick Iranian accent.* People were much more helpful to others who were clearly foreigners than they were to those they assumed to be just out-of-touch Americans.

With these and other culturally clashing experiences under my belt, I soon adjusted my expectations of furlough—instead of approaching the culture with the assumption that I knew everything about it, I took on the same mindset in America that I had had in Iran: when in doubt, ask questions; be prepared for doubt at every turn. "Oh, you're having a cookout? How nice. . .what exactly do people do at cookouts? I would love to bring something, but you'll have to tell me exactly what, because I have no idea what type of food you eat at a cookout."

We spent most of our time trying to develop our support base, which meant that our Sundays and Wednesdays were commandeered by churches in Illinois and beyond.

Our dear boys were not very big fans of the Sunday church-hopping. It was awkward for them to be placed in a strange new Sunday school each week. It was particularly difficult for Steve, who was old enough that he was constantly being introduced to classes as "the missionary kid" and begged for stories of his life in Iran. It was trying on the shy little man, and after just a few Sundays, I began inviting him to my Sunday school classes if he so chose. The last thing I wanted was for any of our kids to feel that their parents' work was a burden.

Steve also entered an American public school for the first time— though we had worked him through the second grade curriculum at home, his English was not yet on quite a third grade level, and he was placed in the second grade classroom. This didn't seem to bother him at all, and I hoped that being a little older than his classmates might give him an extra shot of confidence in the face of this new situation.

God's provision was consistently apparent. We decided to visit a church in California that had been instrumental in supporting the orphanage. One of our churches in Illinois, knowing the cost of travel, insisted on filling the trunk of our 1952 Ford with food so we wouldn't have to worry about buying groceries during the several day journey. When Dick was filling up the gas tank just before we left, he noticed that the tires on the car were nearly bald, but since we didn't have money to buy new ones. We decided to pray our way across the country. It was an enjoyable trip, stopping at parks along the way to let our boys play off their energy and having makeshift picnics on the roadside. The church members in California was gracious hosts, and we were glad we had gone. The week we got home to Illinois, our car had not one, but three flat tires. I was unspeakably grateful that the Lord had allowed us to make it to California and back before they went completely kaput. His attention to small details continued to astound me.

Despite the minor cultural hiccups we experienced nearly every day, furlough was an enjoyable time. I was grateful to be able to spend time serving my mother and catching up with my sisters, and it was good to see supporters and talk about our work. We also found that our ministry focus began to shift a bit. We knew that when we arrived back in Iran, our places at the orphanage and Kohinoor would be filled. Dick was especially excited to branch out a bit and do some more work with adults, and he was actively trying to develop a way to use the radio reaching Iran for the Lord.

Doreen Corley

10 We Finally Beat the Presbyterians

Our trip back to Iran was uneventful. We chose to travel on an actual passenger ship this time, as opposed to the freighter that had first taken us to the field, and we took full advantage of the swimming pool and playroom.

When the ship docked in Germany, we picked up the 9-passenger van that a friend who was studying in Germany had purchased for us and headed to the Iranian embassy to pick up our visas. We were thankful and a bit taken aback that the paperwork had gotten past the leisurely pace and streams of red tape that typically hampered Iranian bureaucratic processes! Then we were off on a several-day trek across Germany, Eastern Europe, and Turkey to reach Iran. Once we learned that driving through the fields of Turkey provided a smoother passage than staying on the roads, the trip was a cinch.

Our arrival back at the orphanage boarding house was practically triumphant. When we pulled up to the street where Kohinoor was located, we were surrounded by gleeful orphans and the delighted Heydenburks, who had taken over the McAnlises place for the duration of that school year. There were kids to hug, stories to exchange, and changes to look over—the Presbyterian hospital had shut down while we were gone, and the compound bordering ours that had housed their ministries was no longer operational. The mission had consequently decided to rent out the three houses on that compound, and Dick and I were to live in one of them.

We were in the middle of unloading the contents of the van into our new home when I heard an exclamation across the compound and looked up to see Tubah running to greet me.

"Tubah!!!!!" I raced to meet her halfway. "I missed you so much!"

"Mommy Kuchek! How are you? How was America? Are you excited to be back?!" Tubah ran out of breath, and I laughed as I tried to sort through all her questions. "Good, good, it was all good! And yes, Tubah, I am so glad to be back!"

"Let me make one thing clear, honey," I continued as we walked arm in arm to our new house.

"What is it?"

"I know that you're making enough with your sewing job to live somewhere else. But Tubah, Dick and I think of you as our girl. Would you be willing to come back and live with us? The boys miss their big sister."

Tubah stopped short, tears welling up in her eyes. "Of course I will!" She threw her arms around my neck. "I was hoping you would say something like that!"

It was so good to be home again. *Wait, is this home?* I checked myself as I prepared dinner in our new house. It was odd to think of it as such, and parts of me still longed to be in America, but. . .Iran was starting to become a part of me.

Our new house was a spacious brick affair with which I quickly fell in love. The running water on both floors provided the foundation for my enjoyment of it, and the arrival of a real gas stove a few weeks later, courtesy of a new missionary couple, nearly put me over the moon. Of course it took about four months before we were finally able to hook a gas line to the stove so that it was useable, but I was so excited at the idea of using it that those months were trivial.

Furthermore, the house was providentially equipped with a large basement from which Dick could work on his new broadcasting ministry. Dick laid thick carpeting on the floor and 'papered' the walls with plastic. He was in constant communication with TransWorld radio, trying to figure out all the ins and outs of setting up a successful radio station in a place where Christian radio programming was unheard of. ("Finally, we beat the Presbyterians to something!" I told him one day.)

In the meantime, the mission required that we immerse ourselves in 6 months of language study to re-integrate ourselves into the culture. Part of

Dick's cultural refreshers came through an exciting new opportunity he and Mr. Mirzai spearheaded. While we had been in the States, we had picked up a battery-operated projector and a bunch of film strips that illustrated the life of Christ, and Dick and Mr. Mirzai began taking weekend trips to various villages around Iran to show the film strips. Many of the villages had never so much as heard of a moving picture before, and they were in awe of the new technology. Entire villages would turn out to watch the 'movies' and the curiosity and discussions that were brought about as a result of those trips were invaluable. The two men were also eager to get involved in meeting the practical needs of people in the villages, and would help them with such tasks as setting up filtration systems for clean water. Mr. Mirzai, relational and warm, was a favorite among the villagers, and Dick gained beneficial, "hands-on" experience in Iranian village culture as a result of his experiences there.

In true missionary fashion I found that for my part, unexpected responsibilities cropped up to demand most of my time, in addition to which, Steve came down with rheumatic fever and was unable to leave his bed for two months. We were blessed to have an American-trained doctor in Kermanshah who was able to assist in nursing him back to health, but the recovery process was incredibly draining for the poor boy. We tried to make the most of it, and he became an avid reader and chess player during his time in bed, but it was hard for me to watch my little boy suffer.

We were never at a loss for missionary adventures. One day I walked into the kitchen to catch Tim taking a swig from the coffeepot in which we, like all good Iranians, stored the kerosene we used to refill our stoves. My heart rate had never shot as high as it did in that frantic trip across town to the doctor. Tim, true to the plucky personality that was already starting to manifest itself, was totally fine, and easily the least ruffled person in doctor's office.

In addition to raising (or, in Tim's case, corralling) my boys, there were the educational opportunities I had—teaching English at the Iran/American society in town, teaching Steve on his good days, leading a ladies' Bible study, and teaching Sunday school as part of the teacher rotation at Kohinoor.

To Persia, With Love

July 4, 1962

Dear Mom,

  Happy Independence Day! I hope you all were able to get together today. Are you having a cookout like we did last year? Thanks for your letter. We really love to hear from you.

  The boys keep growing all the time. While he's still a little sick, the fever doesn't seem to have slowed Steve down at all. He's definitely the leader of the pack of kids here (though I should add that Tim is usually the one leading them into mischief!), and he regularly beats us all at chess. David and Tim are both well. Tim, as you know, is incredibly curious and generally. . .well, he likes to figure things out for himself, sometimes with 'interesting' consequences. Davy is still a sweetheart, content to play or read on his own most days.

  Now that we're not running a household of 25-plus, we've been getting to know our neighbors a bit. Oh Mom, the neighbors are enough to drive you wild! No, that came out wrong. . .well, I don't want to re-type the whole thing. But what I meant to say is that Iran is. . .time-free. Clocks are ornamental at best. In fact, Iranians are so blissfully unaware of time restraints that you can hardly interrupt them, despite your best efforts! Honestly, like I told you on furlough, it was really frustrating for me at first, because I would have a to-do list, and end up not accomplishing any of it because of a constant stream of neighbors! But one day, right after we got back, when I was complaining to the Lord about it, he reminded me that I'm here for the Iranians. Not to-do lists. It's so easy to get my priorities mixed up sometimes. Anyway, though, now that I've learned what to expect in any given day, I've found that chatting with my neighbors is one of the joys of my day, and if someone doesn't show up, I'll pack up my boys and go interrupt a neighbor. No matter where I go, the hostess already has water boiling for tea and snacks set out on a plate for me before she even opens the door! It puts me to shame, it really does. Iranians consider guests to be gifts from God, and I pray daily that I too would be able to see them as such, even on my busy days.

  OH! Mom, you'll never guess what happened yesterday. I'm not sure you would want to! We'd been hearing noises above our ceiling for quite some time, so I finally sent some of the Kohinoor orphan boys up there to figure out what was going on. Mom, would you believe, we had. . .I would hate to say hundreds, but many, many pigeons living up there! So before dinner, everyone went up to the attic for a pigeon hunt. A bunch got away, but we killed 47 of them, and I cooked some of them for dinner. They were very tasty. I *bet you never imagined that your daughter would use your shepherd's pie recipe for pigeon, did you?!*

I must be off—we're packing up to go on vacation to the Caspian Sea again! Give my love to the girls and Don and the kids. I miss you all.

Love,

Doreen

Following the long winter, a group of the missionaries in the area took another vacation to the Caspian Sea. We found a caviar factory on our trip down, and when we stopped for a visit, we received a free tour, complete with caviar samples. The children were decidedly underwhelmed by the strong taste. While Dick and I were not partial to it, either, we did have a laugh at the thought of the "poor, underprivileged" missionaries enjoying world-class caviar while on vacation at the Caspian Sea. "Our supporters would probably be far less impressed by our sacrifice if they saw us now," I chuckled to Dick, making a face at my second taste of the fish eggs. Familiarity failed to make the heart grow fonder.

When we got back from vacation, my fall schedule took on an additional load as David started kindergarten and a nearly recovered Steve began his fourth grade studies. Dick and I finally took exams for our required post-furlough six month language study (nearly a full year after we'd returned to Iran!), and Dick continued his work evangelizing in surrounding villages and running the radio station.

Corley Courier

Box 5

Kermanshah, Iran

September 1962

Dear Praying Friends,

"For nation will rise against nation, and kingdom against kingdom, and in

various places there will be famines and earthquakes." Mt. 24:7.

I decided to write an extra edition of The Corley Courier this month, realizing that many of you heard the news and are concerned for our welfare. On Saturday night, Sept. 1st, an awful earthquake struck, affecting about 75 villages. Because of the way the houses are constructed (frequently out of mud or shoddy materials) and the severity of the quake, many villages were completely flattened. The stricken area was to the north of Kermanshah so we didn't feel anything at all, but Dick and Omer Burris made a trip to the scene, spending two days there. From one village only 210 survived out of some 430 occupants. One man lost 20 members of his family. Most of the folks were in a state of complete shock, beyond tears, and could say without any trace of emotion, "There's my house; my wife and children are under that pile of rubble." Thousands of souls went out into eternity without any knowledge of the Saviour. The re-building will take years. We are praying that God will provide physical and spiritual relief to these people.

Our fall schedule begins next week. Dick's will include hospital visitation and showing evangelistic movies there; Friday morning class for those wanting to be baptized; Friday afternoon class for young men (studying Mark at present); showing films in the church on Wednesday and Thursday afternoons and doing the translation for these films; working in the bookroom; passing out literature; and continuing his village trips with the films. My work will include visitation (which I have greatly enjoyed these past weeks); women's meetings on Tuesday; a teacher training class for Sunday School teachers; translation of a Bible Course; and last, but not least, teaching my own two boys school—which occupies me all morning. We're obviously very busy! Won't you please pray that through these means some might find Christ?

Because of various delays our trial tape has not gone off to the radio station yet, but I think we can safely say that by the time this reaches you, it will have been sent. How we pray that soon the gospel will be coming into Iran via radio! Are you still praying?

I sighed as I typed the final sentence. My heart was burdened. The September 1st earthquake had thrown our purpose in Iran into sharp relief against our day-to-day activities. While I knew that my calling in Iran included things such as mothering my boys and participating in neighborhood teas, the urgency I felt to introduce Jesus to the myriads of people I encountered every day weighed heavily on my heart, and I desperately hoped our supporters were participating with us through their ministry of prayer. I needed those prayers myself, for the spiritual and physical needs in Iran that had been highlighted by the earthquake were overwhelming; my sense of urgency for spreading the Gospel, while fueling my work, was also draining. I could only hope that prayers for our ministry and encouragement had not been buried under the avalanche of daily "to-do" lists that probably overwhelmed our supporters.

The radio station formed a clear bright spot in our ministry. Our dreams for it were speeding to fruition and on November 6, 1962, I excitedly wrote my mom that at long last, "we're on the air!" Our first program was only 15 minutes long, but it was a start. Two young Iranian Christians worked alongside Dick to put on the regular programming, and with much prayer we were able to raise the 200 dollars a month we needed in operating costs. The far-reaching potential of the radio ministry seemed to breathe new life into Dick, and I enjoyed watching him pour himself with vigor various ministry tasks and exercising his gifts.

'Oh Yes He Cares'

We settled back into Kermanshah comfortably, but I knew that I had acclimated fully to missionary life when I found that I was bracing myself for the next round of big change. I found it difficult to trust in anything that felt like routine. Things on the field were too often disrupted. I was right—we found out in March of 1963 that we would be heading to Tehran the following fall to open up a boarding house for the children of missionaries. There was a wonderful English-speaking college preparatory school in that particular city to which missionaries were eager to send their children, but the cost and relocation concerns were prohibitive unless an inexpensive housing option was made available. We therefore began preparing for our next move, this one to the largest city we had lived in to date. Not being much of a city person, I was not thrilled by that aspect of the news, but I did enjoy playing a role in starting a ministry.

Tehran offered more than just the bustle of city life as a cause of concern; the Shah of Iran had been fighting civil tension for several months, but now things were starting to reach a breaking point. Most of the problems swirled around the Shah's biggest denouncer, a man named Khomeini. As a *mullah*, or holy man, Khomeini had always had a great deal of power over the minds of the Iranian people. As early as 1944, he had begun to speak out against the monarchy, for the Shah's army had killed Khomeini's father many years before. He led demonstrations against the Shah's modernization program in 1963, and by the time we reached Tehran, the Shah had decided to fight back. He arrested Khomeini in a city called Qom and exiled him to Iraq; the people, who largely supported Khomeini, rioted in Tehran. While Iranians had no problems with Americans, per se, the American embassy warned us to stay off the streets in order to ensure safety. Dick and I were not too concerned—we knew that the Iranians were able to separate international politics from individual people, and even if America had been involved, our Iranian friends and neighbors would have seen to our safety.

Into this madness we descended with a group of homesick elementary and middle-schoolers. I was nearly six months pregnant with our fourth, and in between settling into the house, mothering the kids, soothing the parents who had come to drop off the kids, and taking care of my own brood, I had my hands full.

We had been blessed to find a house that fit our needs perfectly; located just off a main street, it was a 15 minute walk from the school and had a beautiful backyard filled with fruit trees that helped me resign myself to the fact that I was living in a city.

November 4, 1963

Dear Mom,

Well, once again, the best laid plans of mice and men have gone awry. I know I've owed you a letter for several weeks now, but I've barely had a chance to breath! The boarding kids all seemed to catch a homesickness bug after the newness of the place wore off, so October was hard on all of us. But I think we're past the worst, and now we're counting down the days until the new baby. The kids cannot wait! They helped me set up the nursery, and are always making suggestions for what to name the baby—of course, most of the suggestions are "Why don't you name the baby after me?!"

Yesterday I—

I stopped typing as a sharp cramp pierced my side. "Ooof." I grunted, holding my side. *Uh oh. The baby isn't due yet.* I stood and paced the room, taking deep breaths, but the pain didn't stop. Turning, I saw blood on the carpet behind me and froze. *I have to get to the hospital!. . .How?* Dick was out running errands to who-knew-where, the car was in the shop, our cook was on his monthly 4-day trip to see his family, and I certainly couldn't walk to the hospital. We didn't even have a phone. I was stranded. Fighting back tears, I crawled into bed.

A few hours later, I suddenly heard a clatter of feet and general hubbub as the kids got home. "Phoebe!" I called out, trying to steady my breathing. "Will you come here please?"

"Mummy Kuchek, there aren't any snacks re—what's wrong?" Our Faraman-raised helper rushed to my side when she saw my face.

Not wanting to alarm her, I forced myself to speak evenly. "Phoebe, honey, I need you to take care of the kids. There are cookies in their usual tin, some *dolma* left over from last night, and. . let's see, I think there's some *dugh* that is about to go bad," I said, referring to the kids' favorite yogurt drink. "And then you may have to make dinner, as well."

"But Mummy—"

"I was planning to make *lubia polo*." I continued, ignoring her wide-eyed concern. "You know how to make that, right?"

"Of course, Mummy Kuchek. Just mix green beans, beef, rice, add a little tomato sauce. . .but what—"

"That's right." I gritted my teeth as another pain hit me.

"Mummy Kuchek, what can I do?" Phoebe cried out, wincing along with my pain.

"Nothing, honey." I told her. "Dick will be home very soon, so just send him up to me, please. And don't tell the kids anything. I don't want them to worry."

Phoebe nodded and walked out slowly, glancing back at me and biting her lip.

In just a few moments, I heard Dick's step outside our door. "Dick!" I called out. "Honey, we need to go to the hospital." I lowered my voice to keep the kids from hearing.

"What's wrong?" Dick rushed to my side.

"The baby—I'm scared. . ." My voice couldn't squeeze past the lump in my throat.

"I'll get a taxi," Dick said in a tight voice, out the door almost before his words were out of his mouth. Several minutes later, he re-appeared carrying my coat.

"Come on." Slipping an arm under my shoulders, he hustled me out the door to the taxi. The taxi driver must have known it was an emergency, and he nearly broke world records on the way to the hospital. There were no shocks on the car, and I had to bite back a scream each time we hit a bump. By the time we got to the hospital, I understood, even before the doctor could say anything, that nothing could be done. The child, our first girl, was stillborn.

I wept in Dick's arms. "Dick, I wanted a girl so badly." He turned his head to catch my whisper and gently stroked my hair, his own eyes welling with tears.

"I know, sweetheart, I know."

Dick stayed with me long enough to help me move to a recovery room. The kindly doctor ensured that I was placed at the end of the labor and delivery hall so that I wouldn't have to see or hear newborns as I recovered. My husband departed to face the difficult duty of telling the children that no new baby was forthcoming. (They promptly christened the girl "Angel".) Dick and another American missionary man buried our Angel in the international cemetery in Tehran a few days later.

Why, Lord? I sobbed alone in my room that night. *Why? I've wanted a girl for so long. . .and so many people in Iran don't even* want *their daughters! Why not allow Dick and I to have that girl?* As my harsh sobs finally began to soften, I felt the Lord reply, not with answers, but with the same song I had recalled on the night my father had died.

Does Jesus care when I've said "goodbye"

To the dearest on earth to me,

And my sad heart aches till it nearly breaks—

Is it aught to Him? Does He see?

Oh, yes, He cares, I know He cares,

His heart is touched with my grief;

When the days are weary, the long nights dreary,

I know my Savior cares.

As I played the words over in my head, I knew—he wasn't necessarily going to take the pain away, not while I was on earth, at least. But he offered me the hope and strength to bear it.

11 Snapshots of the Life of a Boarding Mom

I was in the hospital for a few days, but as soon as I got home I threw myself into my work, determined not to let my pain rot into depression. One of my first priorities, of course, was the children. For weeks before they arrived I had been praying about how I would steward them. *If my boys were away at school, what would I want from their mother figure?* I decided that one of the most tangible goals I could set was to be home every day when the children came home from school, for in that first ten to twenty minutes, I was able to learn more about their days than at any other time. Not being above a little bribery, I set up a special afternoon snack time for the kids so that nearly every afternoon when they came home I was there to greet them with tea, cookies, hugs, and questions about their days.

It was quite a challenge to run a houseful of children with anything akin to efficiency. We had just gotten a television set, and I allowed the children to watch one hour a day after they had finished their homework. We only had two stations, one Iranian and one American, but the arguments that could ensue over those two options were enough to make a grown woman cry (and on occasion, they did). I finally made the rule that if I heard the slightest hint of an argument pertaining to television, the set would be turned off for the rest of the day. From that point on, the children became either very cooperative or experts at arguing quietly so that Aunt Doreen couldn't hear. Either way, my objective was achieved.

On Oxen and Children

All the kids were assigned chores around the house in addition to keeping their rooms cleaned. While I had hired outside help, they mainly helped me do prep work for cooking our large meals and did the more difficult tasks of house maintenance, such as cleaning the oven and bathroom. The kids were in charge of keeping the yard clean, washing the dishes, and keeping their own rooms and the general living spaces tidy. The tidiness, or lack thereof, of the common areas was a constant source of tension between the children and me. It seemed that every time I looked around, the common areas were strewn with books, jackets, toys, socks—whatever the children felt the desire to discard at that particular place. After months of alternately begging, threatening, and nagging the children to keep their stuff in their rooms, I finally devised a lost and found system. After gathering up all the things strewn about the common areas, I told the children that anything that was left out would be designated to the lost and found box, redeemable for a price. It was a fairly effective system, as far as it went, for the children hated parting with money (though this sometimes meant they were willing to part with crucial articles of clothing, like winter coats, rather than paying me the few *rials* it would take to redeem said coats). The only downside to the system was the impact it had on my relationship with the kids. They constantly complained about it, I became more stubborn in response, and it sometimes seemed that all we did was butt heads.

One day after I had packed the children off to school, I settled down to read my Bible for a bit before starting the day's chores. I happened to be reading the 14th chapter of Proverbs that day, and when I came to verse 4, I stopped short. "Where no oxen are, the crib is clean, but the profit is in the oxen." As I re-read the verse, my mind translated it thus: "Where no children are, the house is clean, but the profit is in the children." *Oh no. Lord,* I realized, *I've been trying to keep an American house in an Iranian context, and I've totally missed out on the blessing of the children You've given me to care for. I am so, so sorry.* That attitude adjustment proved to be one of the most critical I could have made—my relationships with the kids improved ten-fold from that point forward.

Family Fun Times

As at Kohinoor, Dick and I tried to keep life at the boarding house entertaining for the children. While school and homework kept them busy most nights, we also made sure that we did things as a 'family' unit. Once a week, for example, we would all gather to watch a famous Iranian comedy, *Khoneh Beh Doosh*, on television. Even the children who didn't speak Farsi well found it hilarious, and nobody ever wanted to miss it. On weekends, after the children cleaned their rooms and I inspected them, we took picnics outside the city or hiked in the mountains. Some Fridays I would lift the limit on television so the children could watch *futbol* to their hearts' content.

Our beloved Caspian Sea was only 3 hours away, and many Saturdays we would wake up early in the morning and set out to spend a long day at the seaside, coming back sunburned and pleasantly exhausted.

Dick and I were also careful to protect our time together as a couple, and one morning a week, after the children were at school, we would take a picnic outside the city and spend time enjoying each other, praying for one another, and sharing our joys and struggles with each other. (We always got home before the children did, and they never knew about the picnics, for we wanted to avoid the inevitable outraged cry, "YOU WENT ON A PICNIC WITHOUT US?!?!!!")

March 24, 1964

Dear Mom,

Well, I got as far as the greeting when I last sat down to write, but it's now March 28th, and if I don't sit down and write you now, the month will be gone entirely!

How are things at home? Did you get the check we sent last week? Let us know if that doesn't help cover your bills this month, and we'll send another as soon as we can.

We just had a wedding here—Kathy Walker, one of our single missionaries, met a Peace Corps worker here, and they decided to get married and finish out both of their terms together. They were planning on just doing a civil ceremony here and then a 'real' one when they got back to the States, but I wanted her to have something special on her wedding day, so I made a 7 tier cake. You might wonder why I would tackle such a feat; I certainly did when it started slipping! But we slapped on so much icing that it eventually had no choice but to stick.

Have I ever told you about weddings in Iran? They're totally different than in America. They actually start with the engagement—you know how in the Christmas story, Joseph was planning on divorcing Mary to end their engagement? They are similarly serious occasions here. The engagement parties are wild! First of all, the families invite everyone. They take their parties seriously here, as their social status kind of depends on how extravagant their parties are. The girl wears a white dress, and the mullah, *the holy man who officiates, reads off the list of gifts the groom has given the bride (he, of course, works really hard to make sure he gives an impressive list!)*

Then the mullah asks the girl is she's willing to marry the man (whom she may have never met before!), and she is not supposed to answer until he asks her the third time. It wouldn't do to seem too eager! The bride and groom-to-be then go to an official office and sign a piece of paper saying they are getting married. And at that point, they are 'married,' but they don't live together until the marriage supper. Mom, it's so biblical you can't believe it! It's just like the Church is the Bride of Christ, but won't live with him until he comes back and takes her to the wedding supper. Anyway, after that point, the groom and bride live separately while he gets the wedding supper together. It can be anywhere from weeks to years. These parties are incredibly expensive—people on both sides of the family may be in debt for years after the wedding. So the groom saves the necessary money and eventually he comes back and gets the bride and takes her to the wedding supper at his father's house. He can come anytime, without warning, and she'll drop everything and go with him. And then they're finally officially married, and they can live together.

I really did not intend to go into all that, but I thought it might be an interesting glimpse of the culture for you. But now I'm out of time to write—I'll try to get a chance to write you more about our life before June rolls around. I still can't believe how quickly time passes here!

You are in my prayers.

Love,

Doreen

My life seemed to be getting busier all the time. Since we had such a large home, we became a sort of unofficial guest house in the Tehran area for anyone who needed to stop by for anywhere from a few days to weeks. The constant stream of visitors was hardly a bad thing, though at times I felt a bit overwhelmed. One day during the summer of 1964, we came back from house-sitting in the city of Ahwaz to find 40 people having a conference in our home. It had been the most miserable 'vacation' in the world, as Ahwaz, far south of Tehran, was sweltering in the summer. When the temperature had climbed to the triple digits, we were more than ready to return to our home. Walking in the door to find the conference was quite a blow, and I retired to bed hastily, scared that if I stayed around too long, I might say or do something I would regret.

I only had to 'deal' with hospitality for a short while thereafter, however. Two days after we arrived back home in Tehran, Dick came hurrying into our bedroom, where I was doing our final unpacking.

"Doreen. . ." His voice trailed off uncertainly, and I looked up, alarmed.

"What's the matter, Dick?" His face was inscrutable. *Please, not the boys.*

"Our landlord just came to the door," Dick said. "He said we have to move out."

"WHAT?!" I had been mentally rehearsing the possibilities, but this hadn't made the cut. "Why?!" I loved our beautiful home. The fruit trees in the back, the proximity to school, the beautiful courtyards and airy rooms—I hadn't anticipated leaving anytime soon.

Dick sighed. "Well, apparently at some point while we were gone someone let a dog into the house. It's unclean now. No one can ever say their prayers in it again, so the landlord is hoping to turn it into a school, instead."

"Unclean? Dick, did you tell him we don't mind an unclean house? Did you show him the living room?"

"I did—tell him, that is. But he's adamant. He's really upset about it."

I sat down on the bed, taking it all in. "Dick, when do we need to leave?"

"Immediately." Dick tightened his lips. "We have days, at most."

"Dick—how? How are we ever going to find a new place in *days?*" Tears started welling up in my eyes. I hated moving, hated leaving pieces of my heart and precious memories behind—but it couldn't be helped.

Dick, ever the man of action, headed out to find a new home while I turned to household chores and prayer to help stabilize my reeling emotions. By the time Dick came home that night, I had composed myself enough to be able to put on a brave front for him. It certainly wasn't his fault that this was happening, and he needed support just as much as I did.

Lord, I just don't know about this, I thought as I scurried from one room to another, helping Steve and Davy pack and stumbling over Tim. *What are we going to do? We need a place to stay—the boarding kids get in next week! Lord, what are we supposed to do?* Psalm 91 drifted into my panic-ridden mind. "He will cover you with His feathers, and under his wings you will find refuge;

his faithfulness will be your shield and rampart."

Doreen, remember the dollar? Remember the groceries? When have I left you on the street?

You're right, Lord. I'm sorry. You haven't. I know You'll provide. Um. . .but could You hurry, please?

He did. In just two days, Dick had found a beautiful home for us. While the location on the edge of town would make for a 20-minute commute to school, the house itself was above and beyond what I could have ever hoped for; the large, two-apartment house was surrounded by a lovely walled courtyard where we could all sleep in the hot summer months, plus it had a swimming pool and was even cheaper than our old house had been! The best part though, was the long balcony running along the second floor and overlooking the pool and garden. Each morning I spent time with the Lord on that balcony, and thanked Him for that breath of fresh air— when I was up there, I didn't feel as though I was in the city at all! It amazed me that He had been so mindful of the ultimately insignificant craving I had for the country. And once we had unpacked and properly distributed the belongings that we'd stuffed indiscriminately into suitcases, I found that I liked this house even better than our last. *Once again, Lord, You were right.*

Shortly after we moved into our new house, we found ourselves developing relationships with the American military personnel who were stationed in Tehran. As Dick and I got to know some of the families, we also felt the need to start a church in order for the children to have access to Sunday school, and we accordingly set up Tehran Pars Bible Church for the missionary and military communities in Tehran. Dick was able to exercise his gift for preaching, while the recently-arrived Joel Slaughter taught the adult Sunday school and Sara and I took over teaching the children.

Dick's passion, though, was still centered on the Iranian people. Now that our primary ministry was to expatriate children, we were less involved in the Iranian community than we had been back in Kermanshah. Therefore, while Dick was a committed and loving figure in our boarding house, he continually searched for ways that both of us could be more involved in ministry to Iranians.

The radio was his first order of business. It was rough going. Reception was poor at the new house, so Dick decided to record broadcasts to send to the Far East Broadcasting Association stationed in the Seychelles Islands. They would eventually broadcast the tapes back into the country, thus avoiding both the reception troubles and the tight hold the government had on our radio station. We hired some young Iranian believers to help us with some of the technical aspects of the broadcasting; they were quick studies, and were a great help to Dick.

We also got involved in the Bible correspondence course that Joel and Sara had moved to Tehran to administrate. There were twelve lessons in most courses, and we would send the recipients the first few lessons with a copy of whatever book of the Bible those lessons covered. When they responded, we would grade the lessons and send them back with a few new ones, along with two blank applications in case they wanted to give information about the course to friends.

An Operation Mobilization team in Iran had given out books that included the correspondence course information, and the word of mouth advertising brought about an overwhelming response. The course grew to thousands within just a few months, and Joel and Sara were swamped. We decided that personal connection would truly help the lessons sink in, and after participants had completed the first three or four lessons, we would begin to visit them on occasion; Dick was thrilled when I was asked to join Barb Fogle, who was the head of women's visitation, to do weekly visits.

"Of course I'll stay home and do snacktime with the children," he promised me. "I want *you* to be able to be involved in ministry to the Iranians, too."

Visitation

"Just let me get my shoes and I'll be ready to go," I greeted Barb at our doorstep on a Wednesday afternoon, our regular visitation time.

"All right. We'll be visiting. . ." Barb scrutinized the list in her hand. ". .

.Ladan today."

"Oh, I remember her! She's been flying through her lessons. And I think she recruited Taraneh, too."

"Do you know where this street is?" Barb pointed to her sheet of paper and I looked at it and shrugged.

"Not at all."

"Oh dear." Barb groaned a little. "I know the general area, but I don't know where it is specifically. We'll just have to keep our eyes peeled."

"Anything better than asking for directions!" We both laughed at the memory of a recent visitation. Not knowing the way, we had asked several people for directions. The first man had pointed us in one direction. An hour later, a second man pointed us in the opposite direction. By the time the third person had directed us somewhere else, we suspected that none of them had any more idea of where we were going than did we. But the urgent need to save face in that culture drove them to point us in whatever direction they thought the house *might* be, with confident reassurances that "just a few blocks down" would get us there eventually. We now preferred to leave for visitations a little early to give ourselves plenty of time to scope out the area ourselves.

"How have things at the house been?" Barb asked as we walked along. Our lives were so very different that we always enjoyed comparing. Barb was a breath of fresh air for me; after being submerged in kids and household tasks all week, it was nice to talk to someone whose pace of life, while no less busy, was a little different.

"Oh, the usual. Two of the girls aren't speaking to each other because of something happening at school, but they haven't told me what yet. Tim decided last week that he wanted to go to school, too, so after the kids left he somehow opened the front door, and off he went. Of course, he went in the wrong direction, and thank God that our neighbor Zeeba met him on her way back from the market. She brought him back before I even noticed he was gone, but Barb, that boy. . ." I shook my head.

"He's so different than the other two," she grinned. "You sure they're from the same family?"

"Dick and I ask ourselves that all the time. The whole time Timmy was exploring the city, David was sitting in the living room, reading a book. Totally content." I sighed. "But I will say, Tim also always manages to get out of his scrapes somehow. He's like a little Houdini."

Barb laughed at that.

"And what about you, Barb?"

"I'm tired. I've had a lot of visits this week," Barb said. "It seems like every time I picked up something to do, my doorbell would ring. I'm almost out of tea, and I just bought some last week! Doreen, do you ever find it hard to put things down and just. . .sit with people?"

"Oh my yes." I paused. "Well, I guess not as much anymore. I think sometimes people are scared to get too close to me because then they'd have to invite us for dinner, and they can't afford to host all the kids. Honestly, I guess I'm a little scared to invite people to dinner, myself, because I don't want them to feel that they have to reciprocate for all of us. So. . .yeah, I guess not as much anymore. But I know what you're saying. When we lived in Hamadan, all the visits started to drive me absolutely insane."

Barb grinned. "It's almost as though they have a sixth sense. And right when you sit down to do something really important, they show up! But," checking herself, "I guess that's what my ministry really is at the end of the day. Sitting with people, listening to them talk about their lives. . .it's just hard to put that in a prayer letter. 'Today, I sat around with my neighbors drinking tea and eating *naan berenji*.'"

"Well, you can explain how delicious *naan berenji* are so they can pray for your waistline," I teased. The rice flour cookies were one of my favorite treats. "But I know it's hard sometimes, especially when you have a to-do list and you just aren't interested in hearing the neighborhood gossip *another* time. Or even, in my case, to feel like if you have to break up one more argument, or find one more lost shirt. . .it does seem really far removed from this 'all-important Kingdom work' I came here for sometimes. But. . .I guess this is one of those things we endure for Christ's sake. The little annoyances, I mean. The feeling that we aren't able to make a difference. The frustration over the. . .the *littleness* of what we feel called to do right now. I know it's not beatings or persecutions, per se, but it can be hard to not feel like we're making a difference. But I guess that's what we're called to for now. For whatever reason, this is where we've been placed to make a difference, somehow, through breaking up arguments and eating *naan berenji*." I paused, lost in thought, then glanced at Barb. "I've thought about this a lot. Sometimes it helps me get things in perspective."

Barb nodded and agreed.

My visits with Barb were certainly a highlight. The team participation was crucial—I was able to talk to the married women, while Barb, as a single person herself, was able to connect with the single women better. Whenever one person was focused on visiting the participant, the other would teach Bible stories to the children of the house or sit in prayer. We found that the women had to be more open with their communities about their participation in the course than men did. Because they were not allowed to do as many activities outside the house, their parents or husbands were usually aware of their actions, whereas men could have the correspondence sent to a corner store rather than their own homes. All in all, though, we found that the responses we got were generally positive, if not immediately accepting. There was little suspicion or frustration regarding us or our role, and we were welcomed into most homes with utmost Middle Eastern hospitality.

A 'Righteous' Thief

I had become pregnant in the fall of 1964, and by late spring of 1965, I could hardly bear the heat and started sleeping outside. Of course the kids couldn't possibly sleep inside when this kind of fun was to be had, and the entire household soon joined me, sleeping either on the roof or in the breezy courtyard.

One Saturday morning I came down the stairs from the roof to find Dick on his hands and knees in our bedroom, looking under the bed.

"What are you looking for, my love?" I knew I would probably be able to find it faster—and with better posture.

"My other brown shoe. I can't find it."

"Honey, they were there last night. I know, because I tripped on them," I teased. "It's not under the bed?"

"No. And what's more, I thought I would just wear my black shoes, but I can't find those at all."

"Oh dear." I made a little *tut tut* noise. "Let me go start breakfast, and then I'll come back and help you look." I walked into the kitchen and stopped short. One of Dick's black shoes was prominently displayed on the kitchen counter. *What on—how did that happen?* I thought I had seen every manner of untidiness under the sun, but this trumped them all. The kids had never touched anything of ours, and our Iranian helper, Masumah, would never dream of putting a dirty shoe on the counter. *Has someone been. . .sleepwalking?* It was the only solution I could think of.

"Aunt Doreen!" Gillian, one of our boarders, came running into the kitchen.

"Mmm?" I asked, puzzling over the shoe in my hand.

"My bookbag is gone. I can't find it anywhere."

"Is it in the lost and found?" Gillian was notorious for losing things.

Gillian shook her head. "I don't think so. I had it just last night."

"Where did you leave it last night?" I asked on auto-pilot. We'd had this conversation *ad nauseum*.

"In the living room. . ." Gillian winced slightly. "And I'm really sorry. But I meant to pick it up, and. . .do you have it?"

"I don't, dear. I'm sorry. But I'll help you look for it after breakfast, ok? Why don't you go double-check your room and get dressed, and then come back for breakfast." As Gillian headed back to her bedroom, I grabbed the tin tea canister to begin brewing breakfast tea. It felt far too light. I popped the lid off. It was totally empty.

My stomach sank as I put the pieces of my day together in a flash. "Dick!" I grabbed his shoe and ran with it to the bedroom.

"Oh, where did you find it? And where's the other one?"

"Dick, I think we were robbed last night," I blurted. Ignoring his skeptical expression, I continued. "I found your shoe on the kitchen cabinet. Gillian is missing her bookbag, and the tea is all gone, but I know that I filled it just two days ago."

"I don't like this at all," Dick murmured in the understatement of the year.

I didn't either. The idea that someone could get in our walled enclosure was disconcerting. *And we were all sleeping out there!* "Maybe it was a one time thing," I tried to reassure us both.

The entire household went on a hunt for missing items that day, and I was amazed at all the things that turned up (the kids had never been so motivated to clean the house before). We were still missing quite a few items, though, from food to clothing and random toys, and after I had made a list Dick went to the police station to report them missing. The police gave the response we had been expecting, essentially shrugging it off, and we chalked it up as a loss. Since the thief had taken both left shoes from Dick's two pairs, Dick preached the next morning in his house slippers and one of our American military friends ordered him a new pair through the military base.

We took a poll and all of us preferred to sleep outside and take the risk of death-by-burglar rather sleeping inside and risking death-by-suffocation. After praying each evening for safety, I tried not to think of it too much. It was the only way to gain peace of mind; I knew I was helpless, and figured worry would get me nowhere.

The next Saturday morning, though, we were in for another surprise. Tim came running to me carrying two shoes—one black, one brown.

"Mommy! Mommy! I found them!"

"Oh, honey, were you playing under the bed?"

"No, Mommy. I found them outside."

"Tim, what do you mean? They shouldn't have been outside. Who's been playing in our room?" I hurried to our room, Tim following on my heels. Dick's shoes, one black and one brown, were still sitting under the bed. I looked from Tim's hands to the bed several times, trying to wrap my mind around it.

"Timmy, you found those outside?"

Tim nodded, dropping the shoes by their respective mates.

"Well that's odd. Guess our thief couldn't find a use for two left shoes," I told Tim, smiling.

Dick called him "the righteous thief" when he found out later that day. "How many people will go out of their way to return something that is of no use to them? This man has some integrity, no matter how odd it may be." (We found out later that day that in exchange for the return of the shoes he had accepted our unwitting offering of some fresh laundry which I'd left outside, as well as our iron.)

We had a few more incidents with the thief, but I was no longer fearful, merely mildly annoyed at the inconvenience. While what he was doing was clearly wrong, I couldn't help but appreciate that he lived by a code of integrity, however arbitrary it may have been.

After sending our sweet boarding students home for the summer, I had a brief break before I went into labor on July 28, 1965, and gave birth to Ruth Doreen Corley at the Dr. Varjavand Hospital in town. The very first thing I did when she was placed in my arms was fully unwrap her to make absolutely certain that she was a girl. The 5½ pound bundle of joy was the icing on the cake as far as my babies were concerned—but I made sure I reassured our boys, now 13, 8, and 6, that they *were* the cake.

Ruth and I had barely arrived home from the hospital when I had to begin packing up for yet another move. The current house was ideal in everything but location and taking the children the 20 minutes to and from school, sometimes several times a day, had become too burdensome.

Despite my extensive experience in the art of moving, I still considered myself allergic to the concept. I cried with each move, and since I particularly loved this house, packing it up under the influence of post-birth hormones amplified my already tenuous emotional state. The sight of our new house was not particularly soothing; it was a much smaller affair, spread out between two floors, without an indoor staircase to be found. I could only imagine the nightmare it was going to be to have to walk outside in the middle of a winter rainstorm just to get from the downstairs kitchen to one of the upstairs bedrooms.

It was the best we could do, given our circumstances. It was a study in the impossible to find a landlord of a sufficiently large house who was also willing to take on two foreign tenants with an abundance of children and a constant stream of house guests. After the initial jolting adjustment, therefore, I had to make the effort to choose contentment in the situation, and spent a few weeks actively cultivating my gratitude muscle.

I was amazed at how well-known our kids were throughout the city. The combination of our many moves with the attention that a herd of foreign children garnered made us legendary throughout Tehran. The children were always willing to go on errands for me (though I was never sure if it was out of the goodness of their hearts or because they were so spoiled by the shopkeepers) and moving to the new house allowed them to do far more in the way of little errands around town. I loved that they were able to be independent; even the youngest among them was able to fearlessly ride public transportation or run down to the neighborhood grocery store for me. I felt certain that their confidence and independence would serve them very well when they finally returned to the States; they may not have had some of the basic life skills expected of them, such as the ability to drive a car, but they were so highly adaptable that I had few fears for them on that front.

Soon after we moved to the new house and started school, I realized that we were due for another furlough during the summer of '66, and the scramble was on to find someone who could take care of the children in our absence. Unfortunately, no one was available. Ministries to the Iranians were expanding rapidly, and nearly every other couple was booked for the next several months.

At the end of our ropes, we finally decided to "farm" the boarding students out to different families in Tehran for the '66-'67 school year. This meant yet another move, for we didn't want to pay rent on an empty house for nearly a year. We put our furniture in storage at the house of another missionary, just a few blocks away. Because it was so close, Dick was resistant to the idea of hiring a truck; instead, he decided, we would move our stuff by a much cheaper, more culturally apropos method—by horse and cart. That thought was nearly enough to quell my pre-moving tears as I hustled about trying to find ways to protect our furniture from the jolting ride.

I was only able to watch the proceedings for a few minutes on the day of the move before realizing that it would probably be best for my blood pressure if I wasn't around to supervise. My gut instinct was correct; I was (later) informed that my precious gas stove had tumbled off the cart halfway down the street. At least my blood pressure survived.

Just a few days after that move, we boarded a plane for what I hoped would be a trouble-free flight to America. We had barely settled into our seats when Davy turned to me and asked, "Mom—where's Tim?" *So much for trouble free.* But following the initial jolt of panic, a flight attendant informed us that our adventurous son had scurried up to the front of the plane in order to have a better view of the wings, and all was well in the world again.

We arrived, figured out how to use the pay phone, and were soon picked up by the mission and on our way to a campground in New York, where we would be representing the field in Iran at our mission's month-long candidate school. While it was technically a working vacation, I anticipated taking full advantage of our location in the middle of the woods to gain some much needed rest.

The night we arrived, I heard Dick get up and leave the room in the middle of the night. The next morning when I awoke, he was sitting on the edge of the bed with his head in his hands.

"Doreen, I need to talk to you before the kids wake up."

"What's the matter, Dick?" His face was unaccountably solemn.

"Honey, I don't think you heard the phone ring last night, but it was my brother Paul. My dad--" Dick's voice broke.

"Dick, what's wrong?" I felt cold dread creeping over me. "Is he ok? He's not--" It was my turn to lose my quavering voice.

Dick nodded. "He passed away suddenly last night." He swallowed hard, looking down at the floor.

"Honey--" I reached over to support him, my mind reeling. *How could Harold be gone? He was so healthy! And we were bringing him Ruth!* That thought unleashed a torrent of tears. A few years before, inundated with grandsons, Harold had told each of his daughters-in-law that the first one of them to produce a granddaughter would earn 50 dollars.

Mere hours after Ruth had been born, therefore, I'd sent him the following letter:

Dear Grandpa,

I am here, and I understand there is a reward out for me. I weighed 5 pounds and 6 ounces and can hardly wait to have you hug me.

Love,

Ruth

His response had come in the form of a 50 dollar check. When I'd talked to him on the phone after we landed, his first excited question had been "How's my little girl?!" And now he would never be able to see her. The timing couldn't have been worse.

Dick hurried back to Illinois to help with the funeral arrangements while the kids and I continued to hold down the fort at the New Personnel Orientation. Dick and I both missed Harold terribly; his dry sense of humor and quiet manner had made it easy to love him. We took a few weeks off of our furlough duties to grieve and help Dick's family a bit, but there was little time to rest, for support-raising and church visitations crowded our schedule. The year flew by. I found that this time I was somewhat more astute at re-learning the culture, and avoided some of the more awkward faus pax in which I'd engaged on our last visit.

The kids also enjoyed the furlough, Steve most of all. The Tehran Bible Church had no youth group at the time, and as the oldest kid in the house, Steve struggled with the lack of peers in Iran. East Park Church, which we selected as our home church on weeks when we were not travelling or speaking at other places, became a sort of second home to him. He was active in the youth group and made several close friends, and I had to wonder if taking him back to Iran with us would only serve to hinder him socially and spiritually. While Steve was willing to help out with various ministry endeavors, especially with the Operation Mobilization teams that came through Iran, I was concerned that he felt lonely.

With this question lingering in my mind,, we returned to Iran and set up residence in the house where we had stored our furniture, as the family who had been renting it had moved on. The boarding students were happy to be back under one roof, and I was thankful for a house with stairs located on the inside. We had ten kids that year, six boys in addition to our four, and Ruth and I worked hard to keep the house from morphing into a man's world.

It was not easy. This group of boys was challenging in a different way than I was used to. Davood, the oldest and a recent 'graduate' of the Faraman orphanage, had just begun college, and the accomplishment was going to his head. One day, when I asked him to go to the store to buy bread for the household, he turned to me with a horrified expression.

"I don't think college students should have to buy bread," he informed me.

"Well, Davood," I responded as calmly as I could, "then college students shouldn't have to eat bread either." He chose to go to the store in light of that argument, but it was a constant challenge to work with him. (In the course of our years together, he would come to know the Lord, marry one of the girls from the orphanage, and move to American to pastor a small Iranian church. Knowing the eventual fruit of my labor up front would have been nice, but God had some lessons to teach me about faithfulness in drudgery during that difficult time.)

Aside from attitude-copping college students, I was also in a daily battle against the shenanigans of the younger kids, as I discovered that missionary kids are incredibly creative in their methods of mischief creation.

One night as I sat in the living room I heard a screech of car brakes, followed by a loud thud, and Tim ran into the house with Chris Jaeger, one of our other boys. As soon as they cleared the doorway, they slid to a guilty standstill, panting and pointedly avoiding my eye contact.

"Boys, what just happened?" Anticipating that I wouldn't appreciate the answer, I briefly flirted with the temptation to play along with them and pretend nothing had happened.

"Um. . .there was an accident," Chris began quietly.

"What kind of accident?! Are you boys ok?" I looked at them more closely, assessing for blood and breaks.

"Nope, we're fine."

"So what happened?" I persisted. The boys were masters of evasion, but they had underestimated the prying prowess of a mother many times over.

"Well, Mom, we were. . ." Tim took a deep breath, stared at the floor, and plunged ahead. "We were playing a joke."

Further questioning revealed that the 'joke' came in the form of the boys going outside at dusk, standing on either side of the road, and lying in wait. When a victim drove into sight, each boy would suddenly lift his arms and pretend to be playing tug of war across the road. The driver would brake violently to avoid the imaginary rope, the boys would be thoroughly amused, and everyone would have a rip-roaring good time (minus, I suppose, the hapless driver). This time the prank had gone awry, and the driver, losing control, flattened a small tree outside of our house. Dick went to great lengths to reassure the driver that the tree was of no great importance to us, and that he needn't be concerned with reimbursing us.

I quickly put a stop to that game, but no matter how hard I tried, I could never cure them of pranking our guests. Hosting continued to be a large part of our ministry, and the boys always felt the need to break our visitors in, usually at the dinner table. I had covered the table in a large oilcloth, and the boys quickly discovered that the edge of the cloth, when flipped upward, worked exceedingly well as a trough. Shortly after a company dinner began, one of them would slyly flip up the edge of the cloth in front of him, and the others would rapidly follow suit. The ringleader would then pour some of his water into the trough and all of the conspirators would tilt the cloth just enough to send the water flying into the lap of whomever was not quick enough to catch onto the prank. Dick and I protested this act at first, but after we had gotten doused a few times, we took a more defensive role and just watched the boys carefully during dinner so we would know when to flip our end of the tablecloth.

12 Going on Someone Else's Honeymoon

While most of the roles Dick and I assumed upon our return were ones that we were very much used to, we found that there was also an entirely new role to take on: three of the orphan girls who had lived with us at some point, Javahair, Phoebe, and our dear Tubah, had become engaged while we were on furlough, and they each wanted us to play a role in their weddings. Dick and I were delighted to be able to fill in as their parents, and I offered to help plan the weddings with relish. In my interactions with our girls, I tried both to guide them in wise decision making and to model a healthy relationship to them through my interactions with Dick. It wasn't hard; Dick was so sweet and thoughtful that I found it a joy to partner with him in life.

I took a particularly active part in Javahair's wedding; she was a little younger than Tubah, and she eventually asked me to officially take the role of her mother throughout the process. I eagerly agreed, especially when she explained that her groom's apartment was too small to host a party, and asked if they could hold the wedding supper at our house.

The next several weeks were a whirlwind of furious planning, and the day of the wedding, I was incredibly pleased with how well everything had turned out. We had blanketed the stone courtyard from one side to the other in thick Persian carpeting; the courtyard was festooned with twinkle lights, which served as both decoration and an apologetic explanation to our neighbors. They would immediately understand the decorations to mean that a very special party was occurring, and Iranians loved their parties enough to let neighborhood disturbances slide if they happened in the name of celebration. The party began after a beautiful ceremony at the nearby Good Shepherd church.

The wedding party relocated to our house; Javahair's groom Jamshid had hired a cook, who had been toiling in my kitchen since dawn that morning, putting together a meal for the 125 guests. By the time the bride and groom arrived, dusk was settling over the whole courtyard, and the scene was beautiful. The kids and I hurried about serving tea to all the guests, and they sipped their tea and snacked on nuts and seeds as the sun finished setting.

Then the dancing began. The wedding guests were primarily Kurdish, and the dancing was heavily influenced by that culture; the men lined up on one side of the courtyard, arms around each other, while the women did the same on the other side of the courtyard. Each line had a leader, who waved a handkerchief and directed the movements. I had always enjoyed Kurdish dancing—it was done with a joy and abandonment that I admired. Unfortunately, I could not join the dancing myself, for it as not considered seemly for a pastor's wife to dance. I could and did, however, support from the sidelines until it was time to serve up the delicious meal. Dinner was served last, as it was almost always the culminating event of an Iranian party, and it was a true testament to the cook's culinary skills.

The party continued into the night, but at about 10:30 or 11:00, guests began to disperse. I was standing near the door saying goodbyes, when Javahair approached me.

"Mommy Kuchek," she said, "I want you to go with me tonight."

I blinked. "What?"

Javahair repeated her request. It made no more sense the second time around.

"What do you mean?" I asked her. *Go on her honeymoon with her? I've never heard of this.* I had been in Iran for so long that social customs normally didn't throw me, but I had the suspicion that I wouldn't appreciate this one.

"We're going back to Jamshid's house," Javahair told me. "And his family, his mother and sister will be there."

Her straightforward explanation seemed to be missing some key details. Trying not to let my concern show, I finally go up the courage to ask, "What am I supposed to do?"

Javahair looked a bit surprised. "You need to verify that I am a virgin. If you are not there, that means that nobody cares whether I was or not."

I blinked again. Her explanation did not assuage my fears in the way that I had hoped. "Javahair, I—I would never doubt your virginity," I told her in a vain attempt to avoid the situation.

"Mommy Kuchek, you must come," she told me gently. "For my reputation, as well as for yours. You raised me. You're my family."

Realizing that all my resistance was futile, I reluctantly agreed and went upstairs to pack up an overnight bag. The wedding guests who remained had packed Jamshid and Javahair into a car for a parade around town, beeping the horn and making a joyful ruckus. When they returned, I got into the car with Jamshid and Javahair and drove with them to Jamshid's mother's apartment.

It was a small apartment on the second floor, and his widowed mother and sister were already awaiting our arrival with tea and light snacks. I longed to go straight to bed, but first we had to open all the gifts, for Iranians very rarely opened gifts in front of the givers. It wasn't until around 3 o'clock the next morning that we finally moved toward bed. It was at that point that I realized how extremely small the apartment actually was. The mother and sister would be sharing a bed in the single bedroom. Jamshid and Javahair would be sleeping in a tiny room that had once been a sort of storeroom.

"Where would you like me to sleep?" I asked Jamshid's mother, hoping against hope that there was another bedroom or room otherwise suitable for sleeping tucked away somewhere in the tiny halls of the apartment.

Javahair answered. "Mommy Kuchek, you need to sleep in the hallway by our bedroom door."

This was far, far worse than I had anticipated. "I *what?!*"

It couldn't be helped. Even if I had wanted to sleep elsewhere, there was simply no other room in the apartment. The hallway it was. The mother made up a comfortable pallet for me on the floor and I was tired enough that it would have taken far greater levels of physical and social discomfort to keep me awake. *It's only one night*, I comforted myself as I drifted to sleep.

That, unfortunately, was false comfort. The next morning, Javahair came out to me and told me that she and Jamshid had fallen immediately asleep the night before. "We were so tired, Mommy Kuchek," she explained. "You'll have to come back tomorrow night."

I walked home and spent the day in a sort of miserable stupor; in all my time in Iran, I had never experienced such acute social discomfort. But I returned to my vigil that night, and the process was over quickly enough; Javahair came out and showed her mother-in-law and me the cloth, ala Deuteronomy 22, and we all agreed that she was, in fact, a virgin. I escaped the house as quickly as I could, and, walking home, resolved that I would find another mother for any of the other orphan girls who threatened to get married. I never wanted to go on another woman's honeymoon again.

13 Tragedy Strikes

The school year passed swiftly, and with its close came another big change in our household. Ever since we had returned from furlough, I had been keeping a close eye on teenage Steve, and I was certain that Tehran was not providing him the spiritual and social atmosphere he needed for growth. He had kept in touch with some of his friends from East Park, the church we had attended while on furlough, and I could tell that he yearned to have peer companionship again. Dick and I wrote to the Paynes, a family who had a son close to Steve's age, asking them if they would be willing to take Steve in for his remaining two years of high school. In many ways, it was an ideal situation; in addition to living with a loving family and close friend, Steve would be able to walk to school and church, and work part-time in the gas station the family owned.

The Paynes' response was prompt and gracious; they would be happy to take Steve! That August, therefore, I said a gut-wrenching goodbye to my sixteen-year-old child and put him in the hands of an Operation Mobilization team to return to the States. As the car containing my son drove away, I knew that the boy I sent away would be a man by the next time I saw him.

"We Still Have Work to Do"

I had assumed that Steve's departure would be the culminating 'sacrifice' of 1968; none of us could have foretold the tragedy that rocked our small missions community in October of that year.

I was making dinner one night, chatting with some of the kids, when the phone rang.

"No, my dad's not here right now," Tim said into the receiver when he answered. "Yeah, mom's here."

I wiped my hands on my apron and walked into the hall where the telephone was located. "Hello?"

"Doreen? It's Alpha." Alpha Heydenburk was housing some of the Faraman children in her home, and called from time to time to trade advice or stories.

"Oh hi, Alpha. How are you?"

"Doreen—have you heard?" Her voice quivered.

My heart dropped. "Heard what? What's the matter, Alpha?" *Surely not Dick?!*

"The Blisses. . .Mark and Gladys were in a serious accident tonight."

"How serious?" I gripped the phone cord and leaned against the wall.

"The kids. . .Doreen, they lost all three kids."

No words would come as her statement assaulted my heart. All three of the Bliss children. *How is that possible?* "How. . .what happened?" I finally choked out.

Alpha explained around her barely contained sobs. Mark had been driving their small car back from a church service. A truck driver had passed the small Volvo without dimming his lights, and as soon as Mark had cleared the truck, he saw a man driving a tractor and wagon across the road with no lights on; Mark had swerved, but it was too late. The three Bliss children and the newborn baby of an Iranian couple traveling with the Blisses had died. The Iranian couple and Gladys were all in the hospital with various broken bones. Mark was battered, but had escaped most physical harm.

Our missions community had never faced a tragedy of this scale before. Our community rallied around the Blisses, but nothing we offered could possibly assuage the pain.

The story circulated rapidly throughout the local community, and we were beset by people offering whatever assistance they could. Watching the Iranians respond to the loss highlighted the differences in our worldviews. The morning before the funeral, the vegetable man paused in counting out change for me and asked bluntly, "Has she gone crazy yet?"

I started. "I'm sorry?"

"The mother. Has the mother who lost her three little children gone crazy yet?" He had no concept of how to cope with death, particularly in such a tragic setting, and assumed that Gladys would not, either.

I shook my head. "No. No, she hasn't." That was practically miraculous, as far as I was concerned. Losing each of our miscarried babies had been heart-rending. I couldn't imagine having had a few precious years with the children and then having them all snatched from me at once.

The funeral was held at the international cemetery where we had buried our own stillborn little girl. Mark stood by the graves, face lined with pain but composed as he waited for a plane to cross overhead so he could be heard.

"Thank you all for coming. I--" He swallowed hard. "People keep asking me how I'm getting through. And the truth is. . .well, it obviously hasn't been easy. But the truth is, it's all worth it." He lifted his head, holding the gaze of his audience. "It's all worth it. We came here to serve Christ, to dedicate a church, and the church will go on. Jesus. . .Jesus is worth it all. Whatever the cost." He hesitated, looked as though he would say more, but then bent over and gathered a handful of dirt to sprinkle over the graves.

"Thank you, Lord, that we got to keep Debbie, Karen, and Mark in our home for a short time. . .and now, thank you for taking them back to your house." His voice was rough with pain, but steady.

I approached him as everyone else headed off to Mark's house. Our baby girl's tiny grave was just a few yards away from the graves of his children. "Mark," I blurted as a wave of sadness and nostalgia passed over me, "wouldn't it be nice to just wait here with them until Jesus comes back?"

Mark looked at me thoughtfully. "No, no, Doreen," he finally said softly. "We still have work to do." I nodded as tears sprang to my eyes. I couldn't imagine persevering so faithfully in the face of such heartache.

I turned and slowly walked back to Mark's house, which was already filled with neighbors. The atmosphere in the house was almost palpable with shared grief. The men sat in the main room, while the woman who weren't bustling around the kitchen setting out the platters of food they'd brought were sitting in a smaller room just off the main one. While Mark, flanked by Dick and Joel, made his way around the main room, speaking one by one to the assembled men, I joined the women. Since Gladys was still in the hospital, I did the honors of pouring the thick black coffee Gladys' maid had prepared. No one took sugar in their coffee, symbolically joining Mark and Gladys in their dregs of bitterness and sorrow.

Weighed down with my own grief, I sat quietly after everyone had been served, sipping my coffee and listening with half an ear to the conversations around me.

"Were you at the funeral?" One neighbor woman asked another

"No, I was making food for today. Were you?"

"No, but my husband was there. He said it was. . .not normal." The woman paused for a sip of coffee, deep in thought. "No one was wailing. Mr. Mark *cried*. But Adel said that he seemed almost *hopeful*."

"Hopeful? How can that be!" The other woman sounded almost offended at the thought.

"I know, I don't quite understand it myself." The first woman shrugged. "Something about his god, I guess. Mr. Mark thinks that he'll see the kids in heaven."

"But how can he be so sure!?" The woman exclaimed. "They were children! They hadn't done anything yet! How could he know whether *Allah* would choose to send them to heaven or not?"

"I don't know. That's just what Adel said Mr. Mark thinks. I don't know what his god is supposed to be like."

I leaned forward and smiled, hoping to catch their eye and enter the conversation.

"Oh, Mrs. Corley! You worship the same god as Mr. Mark, don't you?" One of the women took my bait.

"I do."

"Is he the American god?"

I smiled. "Well, he's the God of everything. But some Americans follow him, and some Persians follow him. . .people from all over the world can follow him. He's not the God of any particular people group."

"And. . .how is he different from Allah?"

"Well. . ." I paused for a moment. "There are a lot of differences. One of the biggest ones is Jesus." The women leaned in as I went on to explain the story of Jesus' redemptive grace as best I could. The idea of being a living sacrifice was clearer to me than ever that night, as I saw firsthand how God can redeem our suffering for his glory.

Full House

We were scheduled for a short furlough soon after the funeral. It was an uneventful but much needed break from the field, and we returned to Iran in September 1970, ready for another round of ministry. We had to rush to find a big enough house for the kids before the semester started, and finally found one across town; yet another move!

I could never quite figure out how the Corley house automatically became a hub of hospitality, sometimes before we had even fully unpacked, and this house was no different. Within a few weeks of setting up house, we had several people living with us in addition to the children, though thankfully not all at the same time; a recent Iranian convert to Christianity who had been kicked out of his house by an angry wife; a missionary woman who was on her way to Pakistan but had some visa problems; American military personnel on their way home--the list went on and on in the revolving door of visitors. The house was in a constant state of upheaval. The kids loved it. Tim made a sign for the front door welcoming people to the Corley Hotel, and the kids were always eager to give up their beds to an unexpected visitor so that they could sleep on a couch or in the living room.

Of course, the steady stream of visitors also made it easier for the kids to sneak in friends from school. I became accustomed to opening the door to the living room to find a few children I'd never seen before sleeping on the floor next to some of our kids.

"But Aunt Doreen, they would have had to take the bus all the way to school early in the morning, and our house is closer!"

"But Aunt Doreen, we had to work on a project!"

"But Aunt Doreen, we were hungry!"

The excuses were legion and unnecessary. I made it clear to the kids that they could have whatever friends they wanted over as long as they were willing to be responsible hosts; an unexpected dinner guest meant that the child hosting would eat less, give up their bed, etc. The kids were good about not testing my limits, and I was pleased to see them all developing a sense of hospitality and generosity.

Dick and I stepped back into our regular list of duties, sending out Bible correspondence courses, doing follow-up visitations, recording and transmitting radio programs, and teaching Sunday school (me) and preaching (Dick).

The Bible correspondence was expanding all the time, and we were hard pressed to keep up with the demand.

We had spent one year in the new house across town when one of our mission couples, the Longeneckers, moved out of our old "house by the kerosene shop", and we decided that it would behoove us to move back to that house in order to be closer to school. I was losing count of our moves.

Because this house was spacious and came complete with a yard for the kids to play in, I went with less complaint than I might otherwise have.

"Mom! Telephone!" Ruth shouted up the stairs one morning.

I stood up, digging my fists into my aching back. I could use a break from unpacking. "Who is it?" Receiving no answer, I hurried to the receiver. "Hello?"

"Hi Aunt Doreen. It's Rick Jones."

"Rick?" I frowned. Rick was Steve's new roommate. After a year at Tennessee Temple University, Steve had decided that he missed Iran, and he and Rick, a fellow missionary kid, had decided to spend their next year at Shiraz University. We had just put them on the 14-hour bus ride to Shiraz the week prior. "How are you, Rick? Is everything ok?"

"I'm fine. I just wanted to call and let you know that Steve and I are at the hospital. Steve hasn't been feeling well, so I brought him here today. The doctor says he has paratyphoid."

I sighed. "Oh dear. Is he ok?"

"Yeah, he's gonna be fine—here, I'll let you speak with him."

I heard the receiver shuffle, then Steve's voice. "Mom?"

"Hi honey. How are you?"

"I'm good." Steve coughed and I chuckled.

"You sure about that?"

"Yeah—I don't feel great now, but the doctor said I'll be 100 percent in just a few weeks."

"Not the way we anticipated this kicking off, is it?" I asked him sympathetically.

Steve laughed. "Nope. Not so much."

"Well, Dad and I can be there at any time," I offered.

"Nope." Steve brushed off my concerns. "I'll be fine. Really. I'm lucky that I'm just now coming down with something like this."

I agreed, not feeling it necessary to remind him of the rheumatic fever he'd dealt with years ago.

We chatted for a few more minutes before Steve said he wanted to get back to studying. "All right, son. I love you. Study hard!"

I was continually grateful that my children had been afforded such quality educational opportunities. Supporters often approached me during furloughs to ask how we managed to educate our children with any kind of consistency. My refrain to them was that God cared far more for my children than even I did, and He was watching over their education. I also never felt it necessary to mention that Ruth had missed kindergarten completely.

One day when I got home from the Bible correspondence office, Dick was waiting for me with a somber face. "Doreen, I just heard from our landlord."

"Oh no." I wasn't sure of the details, but I could fill in the gist easily enough. "We have to move again."

"He's sold the house to another owner, so we have to move. But the good news is, he's giving us free rent at another of his houses until our contract is up." The consummate missionary, Dick saw the financial break as an excellent trade off.

I was less enthusiastic, and one look at the other house nearly made me try to talk Dick into giving up the free rent. It was far smaller than we were used to, with few windows and almost no place to play outdoors. But we could use the extra money, and I had to make the conscious effort to honor Dick's decision to move ahead with the plan. Plus, I reasoned, at our current rate of relocation, we'd be out in six months or a year, anyway.

14 Rest and "Relaxation"

In the spring of 1972, most of the boarding kids went home to celebrate the Iranian New Year, *No Ruz*. We decided that since Steve was in Iran we would take advantage of his presence and go on a working vacation to Pakistan so that Dick could check up on the missionaries there. Besides the six of us, we took Rick Jones and Chris Jaeger, one of the boys we'd boarded for many years. Our VW Combi was fully loaded as we pulled out of Tehran.

The sky was dark with incoming snowstorms as we drove out of Tehran, but we refused to let that slow us down. None of us wanted to give up so much as a minute of our precious vacation time. We had nearly reached the Afghan border by nightfall, and Dick and I, after a quick conference, decided that it would be best to keep travelling to try to outrun any trouble caused by the storms. The Afghan policemen at the border, however, had other ideas. Apparently the snow had caused nearby rivers to flood, and nighttime travel was too dangerous to attempt.

"So what are our other options?" Dick asked the guard. Super 8 Motel had yet to find its way to the Afghan border.

"You can go sleep in the police station," the man offered. No other options were readily available, so we followed his directions to get to the station. When we arrived, we discovered that the small building was already packed with people. I hadn't anticipated that the border of Afghanistan would be such a popular tourist destination.

We finally managed to find an area on the floor big enough to accommodate 8 people, set up a sleep schedule of sorts so that someone would always be awake to watch over our belongings, and settled in for a long and uncomfortable night; on a scale of 'sleeping in 100 degree heat while on vacation' to 'spending the night in a men's tea room on a mountain pass while eight months pregnant', this night ranked close to the latter end. I thought I was used to nighttime noise, having lived with teenagers for so long; this was a different experience entirely. The room was packed and stuffy, and every time I shifted to get more comfortable, I hit one or more members of our party, setting off a domino effect of shifting and grunting that seemed to spread throughout the room.

I wonder how normal people do vacations.

The night dragged, and we were hardly refreshed when we awakened. But when word spread throughout the assembled travelers that the floods had receded, we quickly packed and departed. Arrival in Pakistan meant sleeping in real beds. We were ready for the 'vacation' phase of our trip to begin.

We soon found out that the Afghani policemen's idea of passable roads was different than that of, say, a sane person. The first bridge we came to was submerged under several feet of rushing water. We got out and surveyed the damage dismally. I was ready to suggest that we turn around and go to the Caspian Sea instead, but the menfolk around me viewed the flooded bridge as a thrilling challenge rather than certain death.

Within moments, they had organized a plan to get us over the bridge. Steve and Rick would get out of the van and walk along the bridge next to it, holding it steady so it would not be swept off the bridge into the river. I pointed out the potential flaws in this plan, such as the fact that two young men might not be able to stay on a bridge if a loaded van was at risk of being swept away, but the men were determined to see their brilliance in action.

As far as my men were concerned, 'vacation' had begun with a bang. The Afghan countryside seemed to be made up of nothing but flooded bridges, and we developed a system wherein every time we came up to a bridge, Steve would leap to take the wheel from Dick while Dick and the other boys hopped out of the van and walked alongside it, holding it in place against the flow of water.

My discomfort increased with each bridge we crossed, and though I would not admit it to the boys, I was relieved when we finally came to a bridge that was impassable, as a bus had gotten stuck midway across it.

The boys quickly adapted this scene into their vacation landscape, suggesting that we park the van and join some other stranded travelers in watching the bus. Armed with some light snacks to help us through the show we mounted a nearby hill and waited for the climax of the Saga of the Bus.

The saga lasted a few hours, long enough for the novelty to wear off, and when the bus finally moved, the men were antsy to get going. I took one look at the still-flooded bridge, however, and pulled rank. "Dick, there is way too much water on that bridge. We've already taken plenty of risks today. We really can't risk this."

The boys protested. A few feet of rushing water and imminent threat of grisly death were hardly deterrents to them.

Dick was ready to side with me when we were approached by a nearby truck driver who had heard our conversation.

"This isn't a problem at all," he insisted. "You can just put your van in the back of my truck and I'll drive us across."

His proposal stymied me. It seemed to be at once incredibly logical and totally devoid of sense. "There is absolutely no way I am riding across a flooded bridge in a van on the back of a truck," I told Dick. "I'd rather swim."

Dick cocked his head slightly. "Doreen, you don't know how to swim."

"I'm aware of that." I lifted my chin and stared him down.

He could see that I wouldn't budge on this one. While I hated to disappoint the boys, I felt that I'd taken my daily allotment of risk without complaint, and had to draw the line somewhere.

Steve had inherited my stubbornness. "Mom, there's always a way," he insisted. "What if we just follow in the truck's wake?"

I opened my mouth to veto the idea, but the men of our party were already making plans.

Steve went into full-on director's mode. "I'll take Mom and Ruth," he told the guys. "You guys can get in the truck, and we'll drive across behind the truck; I'll just have to drive fast enough to stay in the wake."

The other guys were in eager agreement, and I knew that I was going to lose this war; I therefore selected a single critical hill to die on.

"Ok, boys, we can do that," I said. "But there is no way I'm going to ride in the van. Ruth and I will ride in the truck, and you boys can ride in the van." It was the closest we could come to a compromise.

The guys decided that this arrangement lowered the odds of the van being flipped over, and we therefore commenced what may have been the most absurd scheme the Corleys had embarked upon since. . .ever. I kept my eye on the rearview mirror the whole time we crossed the bridge, waiting to see the van go flying off the bridge.

In a slap in the face of logic, we made it across the bridge in one piece and continued to the nearest hotel.

I slept deeply that night.

After the excitement of traveling, our actual vacation time was nearly a letdown. It was fun to see our missionary friends, and nice to have a few days off, but I always suspected that the highlight for my boys had been risking all of our lives in the journey. And despite all the distractions, I was reminded of the value of family as we all had a chance to simply enjoy one another's company.

The moderately relaxing family trip was followed by several more months of crammed ministry in a crammed house. The few times I stopped to think about how busy we were, I could hardly make sense of it. Morning and night were packed with our various activities, and I looked forward to our next furlough, scheduled for the summer of 1973, as though it were a lifeline. While furlough traditionally was more stressful than relaxing, I was desperate for some kind of change in my hectic schedule.

Furlough was incident-free, and when we returned to Iran, we were given the chance to move into a larger house; I was grateful for the opportunity, but held the hope of stability loosely. By this point I knew better than to get attached to any particular house.

My Heart's Desire

Just a few weeks after we had moved into the new place, I was given the chance to speak to a group of foreign women regarding my experiences in Iran. They gave me a monetary gift in appreciation and told me to get something I really wanted with it. I was a little chagrined when these diplomat wives asked me what I was going to use the money for, so I brushed off their inquires; but the truth was that the moment I set my hands on the envelope, I knew what I was going to do with it.

"Dick," I announced as I arrived home, "we're buying a toilet."

While I was certainly adept at using the "Persian version" toilet, I had been longing for years to have an American Standard Version, or ASV, and when Dick came home with a second-hand toilet he had found (I didn't ask where) I was beside myself with joy.

Dick hired Abbas, the local handyman, to come the next morning to install the toilet in our small upstairs bathroom. I waited impatiently all morning for him to come, but, true his Iranian upbringing, he never showed up. I finally grew tired of waiting. "Zeinab," I told my cleaning lady, "I need to run some errands. Will you show Abbas where the bathroom is if he gets here while I'm out?"

She agreed, and I hastened out to tackle my various errands. They took longer than I had anticipated, and it was not until several hours later that I finally made my way back home.

Zeinab met me at the door. "Abbas came while you were gone," she told me. "He's finished now."

I barely paused to thank her as I swept up the steps, eager to see the new facilities with my own eyes. I flung open the door of the bathroom. My mouth dropped open.

"Oh. . .oh my." I could hardly take in the sight before me. Planted neatly in concrete over our former Persian version was my new toilet. It was everything I had hoped for, but for one small detail--it was installed backwards.

I was astounded. *What could Abbas have possibly been thinking?* But before I could come up with an answer, my sense of humor caught up with me and I burst into laughter so hearty I had to stagger out to the steps and seat myself before I lost control of my legs completely. The sight of the toilet kept replaying in my mind, keeping me in fresh peals of laughter every few minutes.

The laughter was cut short, however, when I was hit with a sudden realization. *That toilet is set in concrete*! I leaped to my feet and shot down the stairs to call Dick, who was visiting a friend. "Honey, where does Abbas live?"

"I don't know," he replied. "Why?"

I explained the situation briefly. "Where can I find him?"

At his suggestion I scurried off to the *dukon*, or bread store, asking everyone I met if they had seen Abbas. I finally came to a tea house where he was enjoying a late afternoon break and pounced. "Abbas! I need you to come back to the house, please, as soon as you can." I knew that trying to drag an Iranian from his tea was a futile task, and as soon as he assented to my request I turned and trudged home, equal parts amused and frustrated.

As soon as I got home, I ran up the stairs again, just to ensure that I had really been seeing things correctly the first time around. Unfortunately, my vision had been 20/20 in this instance. The toilet was very backwards, the front of it set flush with the wall, and very, very cemented in. As soon as Abbas stepped foot in the door, I dragged him upstairs to survey his handiwork.

"Abbas," I asked him, trying to keep an implied 'what were you thinking?' out of my tone, "look at this. How would you use this?"

Abbas raised his doleful eyes to mine. "I don't even know what it is."

That was a shock. I should have expected as much, but I had simply assumed that since we were putting it over a toilet hole, he would put two and two together. "Well, never mind," I told him. "But you need to pick it out of the cement and turn it around. I need to be able to sit on it; we need room for our legs."

"But if I turn it around," Abbas said, "you can't close the door. The room is too small."

"But you have to." I was determined that nothing would get in the way of my ASV. "It has to fit over the hole, and we have to be able to close the door."

Abbas shot me a look that told me clearly where he stood with regard to crazy Americans and their hare-brained schemes, but he told me that if I left him alone, he would see what he could do.

I left the room without much hope. Perhaps the Era of the Toilet had not yet come to pass.

But I had underestimated Abbas' genius. After much hard work chipping out the hardening cement, he finally managed to manipulate the toilet over the hole. He was right; it was a tight fit, but knowing my alternatives, I wasn't picky. After all that work, I finally had my ASV! "Dick," I told him as we were getting ready for bed that night, "We are going to take that toilet with us every time we move from now on."

My long-suffering husband agreed to my proposal, and ensured that he lived up to it. (From that point on, we took the toilet and my large stainless steel kitchen sink every time we moved.)

But before we moved to another house, we faced another round of change, as David graduated and moved back to America to attend King's College in New York. Though I'd had 'practice' with Steve, it didn't get any easier to give a child up to a land of unknown possibilities, and I spent the several weeks leading up to his departure prayerfully turning David over to God. *Lord, you care about him more than I do. He's yours first. Please take care of him,* I prayed as we watched David drive away with the family who would be taking him to America.

I would later discover how powerfully God used His people to answer that prayer; within the first week of classes, David came down with the mono virus. Rather than leave him alone and miserable in an uncomfortable dorm room, Bill Tarter, the president of our mission, picked David up and brought him to the Tarters' home, where Bill and his wife cared for David through his convalescence.

I did not hear the news until David was mostly recovered, and was incredibly thankful that God had surrounded our family with His own, especially in those situations where I couldn't be physically present for mine.

He continued to provide for our other boys, as well; while Steve spent some time in Tehran working with the youth group, he met a lovely British Operation Mobilization worker named Ginny Reeves, and by the time of our furlough in 1976, they were happily engaged.

15 The Beginning of the End

The next few years carried on in much the same way, a whirlwind of visitors, radio ministry, missionary kids, and various and sundry duties that kept us going from morning to night. Dick and I were particularly careful to protect our marriage throughout the hustle and bustle; it would have been far too easy to relegate our relationship to a back burner in order to accommodate other things, but we were determined not to allow that to happen. We decided early on that stewardship of our relationship and family was as much a part of our ministry as anything we did with the Iranians. After all our years of marriage, I was finding that loving Dick had become more natural. Not always easy, certainly--I sometimes resisted the requisite 'dying to self' that was the only way to fully nurture the relationship. But I kept finding that as I sought Dick's best, even at the expense of my own desires, the rewards I reaped were far beyond what I felt I'd sowed. As I relinquished any demand that Dick love me in specific ways, he was freed to love me well in his unique ways, and the more I appreciated him, the more he seemed to love me far beyond my expectations.

After several years at that breakneck pace, our ministry suddenly shifted as the Bible correspondence course became too unwieldy for our headquarters in Tehran. We were having a particular flux of students from a small town near the Turkish border called Rezaiyeh, and we decided that it would be best for us to move there so that we could more readily visit and cultivate relationships with the students.

A bit of research prior to moving revealed that the city in question was remarkable, for people of five different nationalities had been living there in relative peace for years. Besides the native Iranians, or Fars, we would have an opportunity to reach Jewish, Kurdish, Assyrian, and Armenian peoples. There were already a few churches in that particular city, but no resident missionaries, and it seemed a perfect fit for us; finally, the primary focus of our ministry would be on reaching the unreached!

We invited an Assyrian friend, Josephine, to work with us; her fluent Syriac would be invaluable. The city was almost bafflingly open to Christianity. We were overwhelmed by the response. Our dining room table was constantly elbow-deep in Bible correspondence materials to be mailed; in addition to our regular visits with students, we held a 'Friday school' course for young people at a local church to help reach more people at once. Many weeks we had more than 80 people showing up to these classes, and Dick would teach the older ones while I held down the fort with the 6th-8th graders. We trained six teachers to help us with the Sunday school, and they were an incredible blessing as the school continued to grow.

The work was so fruitful in that particular city that we were soon joined by three other families to help us keep up with the demand. With the help of the Fairchilds, Papworths, and Carters, we were able to to keep up with the radio work and engage in even more visitations. It was a thoroughly delightful, if hectic, time.

We soon realized we needed teachers to educate our own children, and we recruited two expatriate teachers for the five missionary children. They were a godsend, and Ruth developed obscure and fascinating talents like playing the accordion under their tutelage.

In the midst of it all, Steve and Ginny got married. We drove the 15 hours to Tehran, where they would be living, for the ceremony. Ruth and Tim both got to participate in the wedding party, while Dick performed the ceremony. It was a beautiful little wedding.

"Dick," I asked him one night morning over breakfast. "What do you think of making our next furlough a full year?" For the past 11 years we had been going on furlough for whirlwind 3-month stints, which never afforded us the opportunity to see all of our supporters, let alone rest.

Dick was in favor of my idea, and we decided that in the spring of 1978, we would take a year-long furlough (which provided us with the double bonus of attending David's wedding to the girl of his dreams, Kathy Bailey, in June!).

I tried not to let my exciting furlough plans distract me from all the other things on my plate, but I would be home before I anticipated.

To Persia, With Love

On February 3, 1978, I walked in the door just as Dick answered the telephone. "No, Don, she's not—oh wait. She just walked in the door. Let me get her."

I snatched up the receiver, cold dread washing over me. My brother-in-law was certainly not calling long-distance to Iran just to pass the time.

"Hello?"

"Hello, Doreen." Don didn't mince words. "It's Pat. Her cancer has spread, and the doctors don't think there's really anything they can do at this point. We're just trying to make her comfortable." He paused and cleared his throat. "So. . .if you're able to come say goodbye, it needs to be soon."

I finished the conversation and hung up the phone in a fog. Pat had been diagnosed with the cancer six years before; she'd been fighting for so long that I'd almost forgotten that it was a deadly disease.

I felt helpless. Of course I wanted to be with Pat and comfort Don, but we had no money to spend on a ticket. "Dick," I sobbed into his shoulder one night, "I won't be able to say goodbye!"

"I'm sorry, Doreen." His face contorted against his own grief as he pulled me close. "If there was anything I could do--"

I had to resign myself. There was nothing to be done.

Two mornings later, the phone rang again and I answered.

"Er. . .may I please speak with Doreen?" The voice was unfamiliar.

"This is she." I played with the phone cord in one hand while playing "guess the caller" in my mind. I failed.

"This is Pastor Rick, from Grace Baptist Church. Pat's church."

"Oh. Right. Is Pat--" My heart jumped to my throat. Had it really come so soon?

"No, no. She's holding on." Pastor Rick hurried to assure me. "But barely. Listen, Doreen, we think it's important for you to be home at this time. So we've taken up a collection at the church, and we've raised the money for a ticket. It should be enough; we talked to a travel agent who can arrange to buy it."

Tears sprang to my eyes. "Oh. . .Pastor Rick. . .thank you. Thank you so much!"

I flew to Illinois on the first flight I could catch, but it was too late. Pat died 24 hours before I made it home. But the funeral, Christ-centered and hope-filled, offered me a chance to say goodbye, and I was able to spend some time comforting my mother and bereaved brother-in-law, Don. Truth be told, the last six years had taken a toll on Don, and he seemed relaxed, relieved that his bride was finally at rest after six years of pain.

I couldn't take advantage of being home, as much as I wanted to, and I returned to Iran shortly after the funeral to resume my duties.

Last Return to Iran

Our year of furlough was a much-needed breath of air. For the first month, we helped David prepare for his wedding to Kathy, and in June, they married in our home church in Illinois. Right after we sent them on their honeymoon, we packed our suitcases and moved to Kansas City, Missouri to be missionaries-in-residence at Calvary Bible College. Dick had been asked to teach classes, and I was excited for the chance to take a few classes at no cost, courtesy of my spousal discount. Tim and his best friend, a fellow missionary kid named Torry, joined us. We had also brought Josephine from Iran, and it was, as seemed to be our wont, a full house.

We enjoyed the slower pace of life in America, but an ominous cloud was starting to creep over Iran; Khomeini, the rebel banished by the Shah, was quietly starting a revolution through the mosques of Iran as he sent tapes carrying his message into the country. The seed of unrest, once planted, was easily cultivated, and the people began to turn on the Shah. Dick and I had once assumed that with the police and army behind him, the Shah was untouchable, but it was starting to look as though our optimism had been off target.

Our supporters started to ask us on Sundays what our plans were, and we always insisted we were planning to go back, but uncertainty was raising its ugly head. The fall was tense, as we communicated with people back home and eagerly watched the news for every scrap of information we could get about our beloved adoptive country.

And then, as we watched horrified from afar, the government collapsed. The Shah fled Iran in January of 1979, and Khomeini had a victorious return from France. The American embassy issued an order to all the Americans living in Iran to evacuate.

Dick and I were stunned. "Dick, how could this happen? We've been there almost 25 years, and now the biggest thing that has happened in Iran in almost centuries is taking place, and we're not there!"

Dick had no answer. No one did.

As soon as we got word of a meeting at our headquarters in New York, we hurried to be a part of it. We needed the closure, we needed to talk to our friends and figure out what was happening, how to proceed from this place. Almost everything we all owned was still over there; only the essentials could possibly have been packed. I prayed our house wouldn't be plundered; I thought with despair about my precious sit-down toilet and gas stove.

At the meeting we decided to wait it out, see if things 'blew over', though none of us had any idea how such a thing might be possible. But by April it was clear that Iran was in this revolution for the long haul, and the mission headquarters deemed it best to close that field for the time being. Our team was dispersed, some to Kenya, some to different areas in America, but all, providentially, to work with Iranians.

Dick and I were perplexed. We wanted to return to Iran so badly it was palpable, but we could think of no way to make it possible.

In June, Dick and our former field leader Al Huntzinger heard that the Iranian embassy was giving American businessmen fourteen-day visas to enter the country and wrap up their loose ends. Dick and Al took advantage of the opportunity and flew back in hopes of being able to visit the handful of cities where we'd had missionaries and bring closure—pay off landlords, pack or sell belongings, etc.

But Dick was not to be deterred from his one mission—to figure out how to return to Iran. So one day, while he and Al took a break, he visited the local work office and boldly asked the girl behind the desk if we could get work permits to return to Iran.

The girl stared at him, no doubt thrown off by the way his foreign appearance contrasted with nearly accent-less Farsi. "What kind of work did you do when you were here, sir?"

"Well," Dick said, "we worked with a church. You know," he continued, cautiously feeling his way around the answer, "Khomeini and I are in kind of the same work. He works in the mosque, and I work in the church." His logic was, amazingly, successful. The girl promised that a work permit would be issued; Dick could pick it up at the Iranian embassy in America.

I chuckled when Dick told me the story. "Honey, I'm not gonna pack yet," I told him. "The odds that she'll remember are almost as low as the odds that Iran will let us have a permit." I had to eat my words; a few days after Dick returned to the States, he drove to the embassy in New York and picked up work permits for both of us.

We were thrilled but our family and friends in the States were far less so. The situation was admittedly unstable, and they were concerned for our safety. For our part, we tried to convince Ruth to stay with someone in America, but she refused. "Mom, that's where I was born and raised," she told me. "That's home." She even went so far as to say that her Farsi was perfect, and with brown eyes, all she would have to do if someone came to arrest an American would be to throw on a *chadder*, or veil, and pretend to be Iranian.

I understood her yearning to return to her home, but I was also concerned that she know the risks. "Ruth," I asked her one day, "Are you afraid to go back?"

"No. Are you?" She shot back.

I thought for a moment. "Well, the worst thing that could happen is that they could arrest us and execute us as spies, and we'd be in heaven that much sooner. . .does that scare you?"

It didn't. And so it was settled. On August 23rd, Dick, Ruth, and I landed in Tehran and began apartment hunting.

Incidentally, the one we settled on was the very first apartment we'd had with a furnace, and we no longer had to move the kerosene stoves from one room to the next to keep warm. I found this reassuring: however long we were going to be in Iran, God would provide.

We began looking for jobs; we wanted to be as inconspicuous as possible, and working for the government would provide us the opportunity to stay in the country without raising undue suspicion. In a plot twist that could only be orchestrated by a God with a vast sense of humor, the first offers we had under the new Islamic regime were to be Bible teachers in Iran's public schools. All students in Iran were required to study the religion of their fathers, and the school therefore needed to provide Bible teachers to those students required to study it. Our classes were attended by children of the Jewish and Zoroastrian faiths, in addition to Christian and Catholic children. Muslim children were not allowed to attend our classes, but at the request of the children and with the principal's permission, we had the chance to show film strips after school to any children who wanted to attend, regardless of religion. A number of the kids in our school were introduced to the Christmas and Easter stories through that means.

The international school we wanted Ruth to attend was open, though the government had taken over the building and it was now relegated to the building where the German ambassador had worked before evacuating. Some of the American teachers had managed to stay behind on work permits as well, so Ruth returned to some familiar faces. The school had been segregated, per Khomeini's order, so Ruth only knew her 13 female classmates. It wasn't until the end of the year, when they published a yearbook, that she saw the boys in her class.

In addition to teaching at the school, Dick was preaching again at the greatly diminished Presbyterian fellowship and teaching several classes to members interested in baptism, and we each ran Bible studies. The ministry was rich, but the times were increasingly uncertain.

On November 4, 1979, Dick and I were discussing our day as we drove home from work when I heard the word "America" crackle over the radio.

"What did that say?" I leaned over and turned the volume up. Iranian students had apparently taken over the American embassy.

"Oh, that's all." I grinned in relief. "They won't be there long." This exact scenario had played out just a few weeks before for an underwhelming 24 hours, and I expected that their efforts this time would be no different.

As we drove past the embassy, a mere two miles from our home, I leaned forward to see if there was any sign of unusual activity, but nothing seemed out of the ordinary. I leaned back in my seat, unconcerned. *It won't last more than two days at most.*

That was the beginning of the 444 days Iranian hostage crisis (and the abrupt end of my career as a prophet). We weren't sure whether the crisis fueled or was a product of the anti-American sentiment that began a steady ascent in the next few weeks, but either way, we felt the pressure.

One day, when I was in the courtyard hanging our laundry on the line to dry, I heard a mob marching down the street chanting "Death to Americans!" *Lord, please keep them on that side of the wall.* My heart pounded in my ears. It could hardly be a secret that Americans lived in this apartment. The mob passed, but my racing heart took longer to calm. Ruth and I took to putting on headscarves and wearing long sleeves each day when we went out, so as to be less conspicuous. On days when big riots were planned, Iranian friends would call us to say, "You should probably stay inside today, ok?" And still there was no relief in the tension.

The few Americans left in the country were gradually being asked to leave. Schoolteachers, Catholics, and Jehovah's Witnesses were a few of the groups targeted by the government as it slowly closed its iron grip around the country we adored.

One day, as Dick was out buying bread, the shopkeeper asked him where he was from. Dick, treading cautiously, quoted him a Persian poem about how "we are all from one great Jewel." The shopkeeper chuckled.

"That's a good poem. . .but where are you from?"

"I'm from the 'Big Satan'," Dick finally admitted.

The man laughed again. "No, you're not. There are no Americans left in this country!"

Dick smiled back. "There are a few. And I'm one of them."

It took several more minutes to convince the shopkeeper that Dick was American; he finally nodded graciously to concede the point and assured Dick, "Well, we like the people from America. It's just the government that's bad."

I laughed when Dick told me the story that night. "Funny, that's exactly how I feel about Iran!" Despite all the tension and trouble, I couldn't disengage my heart from the people I'd loved, the people I now considered myself to be a part of. But in the back of my mind I suspected that our time in Iran was drawing to a close.

I was right. In July of 1980, the announcement came that all Christian workers were to report to the Ministry of Guidance to "clarify" their visa status. We weren't fooled; in this case, "clarification of visa" and "revocation of visa" were bound to be one and the same. Dick visited the office and returned with the news we'd expected. We had been given 14 days to leave the country. 14 days to pack up 25 years of memories, say 25 years' worth of goodbyes—it was unfathomable.

We put a simple ad in the paper: "Foreigner leaving, selling household goods." The response was overwhelming, and in just a few days, we had sold everything from my precious toilet to our old VW Combi van. After all our moves, I thought I'd learned not to place value in material things, but watching our possessions and all the memories they bore being carried out of our house to who-knew-where, I felt a perpetual sting of tears in the back of my eyes.

"Khomeini, what have you done to my life!?" It was our last full day in Iran, and I plunked down by a few half-packed suitcases and unleashed long-repressed tears. *Why, Lord? Why are you letting this happen? To this land, to these people, to our work. . .to YOUR work?*

My answer was silence. And then as I sat on the floor, head in my hands, through the silence I sensed a deep reassurance. *Trust me, Doreen. Can you trust me?*

Lord, if I didn't trust you by now, I'd be a scoundrel, I admitted. He'd provided far too often for me to have any doubt.

The next day we took our last steps on Iranian soil. As the plane taxied down the runway, I was reminded of leaving America for Iran so long ago. There had been so many fears, so many concerns: would we learn the language? Would there be work for us? Would we be able to fulfill the call we had been given?

The answer, by His grace, was a resounding "yes."

Epilogue

We left Iran in August of 1980 and spent 12 days in Turkey to see whether we could fit with the work going there, before heading to Israel for a 10 days of rest and recuperation.

The time in Turkey proved to be disappointing. We had hoped that we would be able to settle in that country to wait for things in Iran to blow over, but the mission organization eventually persuaded us that Khomeini was not going anywhere. Having realized that if we lived in Turkey we would have to learn another language, we felt discouraged and frustrated as we toured the Holy Land. It was the very first time we had been able to 'walk where Jesus walked', and I wanted to enjoy it, but struggled to push away the nagging worries about Iran and our future.

Two days before we were to leave Israel we found ourselves at Calvary, standing at the open tomb and struggling with deep feelings of loss and confusion. Israel had nearly yielded another opportunity to work with Iranians, but those were Jewish Iranians, with whom we had no experience. Doors seemed to be closing all around us.

We sat in folding chairs, staring at the open tomb, thoughts awhirl.

Well, Lord, what do you have for us now? I asked Him. *You've brought us this far; surely You won't leave us now. . .right?*

A young Irishman sitting on the front row suddenly rose, faced the group, and opened his mouth to sing. His clear, faultless tenor spilled over us as we sat in prayerful attention.

. . .Because He lives, I can face tomorrow, because He lives, all fear is gone, because I know He holds the future, and life is worth the living just because He lives. . .

As I allowed the message of the song cleanse my distraught soul, I felt a sense of deep assurance. Whatever happened, whether it was ideal or not, life would continue to be worth living, because I knew Christ.

We reluctantly headed back to the States, confident in our God, but not the path we should take. Following the initial whirl of debriefing at the home office, I found myself waking up daily in a stupor. The day after we'd moved into a missionary house in Chicago that had 'coincidentally' opened up for us, I woke up with a horrible pain in my left shoulder. As I struggled to come to grips with our new lives in America and my grief over having lost the country of my heart, the pain in my shoulder increased to the point where I was unable to function. I couldn't lift my arm, couldn't write letters, couldn't even lie down to sleep at night. Motivation and energy were at an increasingly low ebb, and finally in December, a doctor in our congregation suggested that I allow him to give me a cortisone shot. The shot itself was the most painful experience of my life, but when I woke up the next day it was as though I'd awakened from a four-month nightmare. Within a few short days I had decorated the house from top to bottom, baked loads of Christmas cookies, and sent frantically-written letters out to supporters. Dick and I decided that I must have been going through a somatic depression, and I was just thankful that it was so easily curable.

The home office provided us with duties in the Chicago area, but when I found out that we were supposed to be doing follow-up with the Summer Training Program contacts that lived in the area, my heart sank. This assignment sounded threateningly long-term. It was nice to be close to our family, and we would enjoy meeting new people, but our hearts were with the Iranians.

Lord, what is going on? I begged to know. Any answer from Him seemed awfully slow in coming.

We decided to take advantage of the many colleges nearby. Dick began teaching missions at Moody and enrolled in a class at Wheaton. We both followed up with students who had been contacted by our missions reps earlier that summer. While the work was fine, we were yearning for our next step to be revealed.

It came in the form of yet another placement in America. The president of Calvary Bible College, where we had been a few years earlier as missionaries-in-residence, showed up at our house one day and offered us a job teaching missions. We finished the school year in Chicago for Ruth's sake, then moved to Kansas City, where Dick started teaching again and I took more classes.

Once again, as kind as the school was to us, we struggled to settle; at the end of that year we were offered yet another position, this time as overseas director of our mission, Christar (formerly International Mission). This would necessitate a move to New Jersey. The job required some overseas work, as we would have to travel to all the fields we oversaw in order to problem-solve, counsel, and help hone each field's emphasis.

Dick and I were excited to finally have a link to the overseas world, but Ruth balked. This would be her fifth school in as many years, and she wanted to finish her senior year in one place. She reluctantly came with us to New Jersey and struggled through one final new school before heading off to Moody Bible Institute, swearing she would never leave Moody for another school (she was true to her word).

Dick and I loved having a connection to the outside world, but our hearts remained restless. We wanted so badly to live overseas again, to be active in teaching and preaching to the unreached.

We continued exploring our options and finally wrote to some workers in Afghanistan, next door to Iran, asking if we could come to open a guesthouse there, or even to teach English. They never responded, much to our disappointment, and though the joy of watching our Tim marry Tammie Quinnett in April of 1986 helped mitigate the disappointment some, we could not shake the desire to be working overseas again.

Finally, in early 1987, after nearly seven years of living stateside, we got a letter from some workers in Turkey. Iranian refugees were streaming into Turkey to escape the regime, and the workers in Turkey were unequipped to help people with that culture, that language. They asked if we would come. Dick and I were ecstatic. Finally, a door was opening, and it was perfect for us! We asked Bill Tartar, the president of our mission, if he would allow Dick to become the Middle East director instead of the general overseas director. That way, we could live and minister to Iranians out of Istanbul.

Bill realized that trying to hold us back was futile. So the decision was made and we wrote a gleeful acceptance letter back to Turkey. (Ironically enough, we received an invitation to Afghanistan shortly after the plans were made for Turkey. Our letter 'just happened' to be overlooked until that time; I was grateful that God had delayed their letter until plans had been made for Turkey—a much better fit for Dick and me).

We married Ruth off to Brad Foreman, a man she had met at Moody, the spring of 1987, and flew to Turkey in November of the same year. In 1988, much to our joy, Brad and Ruth joined us in Turkey, and I was reminded of a long-ago day when we had driven through that country on the way home from a furlough and I'd asked the Lord who would tell *those* people about Him. The answer had been sitting in my lap at the time.

We stayed in Istanbul for eight wonderful years, during which time we started two Iranian fellowships and ran a Bible correspondence course for many of the refugees there. Because we worked with refugees, we found that we were privileged to be a part of building the Iranian church worldwide; to this day, we hear from people who came to know the Lord in Turkey before settling in another country.

We had no plans to leave Turkey, but in November of 1995, the American consul called us in and informed us that Dick was being followed by a group of men, thought to be the Iranian secret police, and that we were to be very careful in our activities. After soul-searching, prayer, and tears, and upon the advice of others, we decided to return to the U.S. We were both nearly 65 years old.

We arrived back in America drained and ready for a break, and were welcomed as missionaries in residence for Columbia International University in Columbia, SC. Dick taught there for four years while I finished my master's degree in Intercultural Studies; but we couldn't get our beloved Persia out of our minds. Through regular contact with the field in Turkey, we finally arranged to visit the field twice each year, in both the spring and the fall, so that we could help teach and grow the Iranian fellowships in that country. God has now raised up a team in both Istanbul and Ankara to work with our dear Iranians. Our hearts are happy at last.

As of August 2013, we have just returned from a two-month jaunt in Ankara, Turkey and are looking forward to continuing to see how God will use us to touch the lives of Iranians in Columba, SC.

Our kids have pursued their various endeavors—Dr. Steve Corley recently retired from a 33-year career teaching high school social studies. He and Ginny have two children, Helen and Matthew, and live in Sumter, SC.

David passed away from a stroke in March of 2008, after a successful career in banking. He and Kathy have two kids, Andrew and Daniel.

Tim's lifelong love of airplanes turned into a career in aviation—he is currently the president of a small airplane company that refurbishes and rents cargo planes. He and Tammy live in Seattle, Washington, with their two boys, Joseph and John.

Ruth and Brad have been working in Turkey for over 25 years, and recently opened a retreat center there. They have two daughters, Becca and Melissa (Missa).

Made in the USA
Middletown, DE
24 October 2014